It's All About Relationships

IT'S ALL ABOUT RELATIONSHIPS

Mastering the Art of Relational Leadership

EDDY ARRIOLA

IT'S ALL ABOUT RELATIONSHIPS
Mastering the Art of Relational Leadership

FIRST EDITION

ISBN 978-1-5445-5193-7 *Hardcover*
978-1-5445-5192-0 *Paperback*
978-1-5445-5194-4 *Ebook*

For Katie, Ben, and Grace

CONTENTS

INTRODUCTION 9

PART I: THE SIX RELATIONSHIPS

1. THE BOSSES 17
2. THE TEAM 29
3. THE COLLABORATORS 59
4. THE COMMUNITY 75
5. THE CUSTOMER 91
6. YOURSELF 105

PART II: THE CARPE FRAMEWORK

7. CONNECT 129
8. ALIGN 143
9. RESPOND 155
10. PRIORITIZE 167
11. EVALUATE 183

CONCLUSION 197
ACKNOWLEDGMENTS 201
ABOUT THE AUTHOR 205

INTRODUCTION

Ask any CEO what keeps them up at night, and they'll rattle off a familiar list: cash flow, strategy, product–market fit, branding, operational efficiency. These are the heavyweights of leadership—the tangible, measurable priorities every CEO is trained to tackle.

But ask why a strategy failed, why a product flopped, why a branding campaign missed the mark, or why operations got bogged down—and the answers shift. Suddenly, you hear about misalignment, poor communication, competing agendas, a lack of trust.

At the core of every major business challenge is the thing no one teaches you how to master: *relationships.*

Here's the paradox. Everyone knows, at least intellectually, that relationships are critical. You can't execute a bold vision without an aligned executive team. You can't scale without a workforce that's motivated and engaged. You can't drive revenue without customers who believe in what you're building. You can't manage investors, boards, or partners without trust.

And yet, relationships often *get treated as an afterthought*—a soft skill to be addressed *after* the "real work" is done.

It's not that CEOs don't care. It's that they're overwhelmed.

Which relationships should take priority?

How do you invest in them without spreading yourself too thin?

How do you build trust without losing authority?

How do you make time for people—without losing time for results?

If you've ever felt like you're constantly pulled in a hundred directions, struggling to balance leadership with the emotional weight of managing relationships—*you're not alone.*

The irony is that the higher you rise, the more reactive you become. You wait for people to come into your office, for emails to pop into your inbox, for a crisis to blow up your phone. Your calendar may be full, but it's rarely filled with the conversations that drive real impact. Instead, you spend your time putting out fires or attending to the loudest voices, while the relationships that could transform your business quietly wither in the background.

And it's not just your professional life at risk.

When was the last time you sat down to dinner with your family *without* checking your phone under the table? When was the last time you met up with an old friend, took a day off, or just breathed? CEOs often sacrifice their personal health and well-being on the altar of success, only to find that the cost of neglecting their own needs is higher than they bargained for.

Most CEOs are trying to juggle too many demands without a clear sense of who or what truly deserves their focus. They're playing defense, reacting to the noise instead of proactively building the relationships that matter. And they're doing it all without a plan, a roadmap, or even a clear set of priorities.

This book is about solving that problem.

INSIDE THESE PAGES

At its core, leadership isn't about strategy, sales, or execution. It's about the *people who make those things possible.*

Every CEO must master six essential arenas of relationships that determine success or failure. In Part I, you'll learn how to build, manage, and sustain these six core relationships:

1. **The Bosses:** How to manage up to those who hold power over your future: boards, investors, regulators, and owners.
2. **The Team:** How to align, empower, and grow your senior leaders, so execution never outruns trust.
3. **The Collaborators:** How to cultivate partners, advisors, and allies outside your company who expand your reach and capacity.
4. **The Community:** How to lead publicly, shaping how your company is understood by media, government, and civic institutions.
5. **The Customer:** How to listen deeply, build loyalty, and create the kind of experiences that turn customers into advocates.
6. **Yourself:** How to manage yourself because if you burn out, lose focus, or neglect your own health and mindset, none of the other relationships will hold.

Master these six relationships, and you create momentum.

Neglect them, and your leadership will hit a wall—fast.

But knowing who to focus on isn't enough. You need a system to manage relationships with discipline and purpose—which is why I developed the **CARPE framework.**

CARPE is a repeatable system for building and maintaining the relationships that matter most:

- **Connect:** Be intentional about initiating and strengthening key relationships.
- **Align:** Ensure that expectations, incentives, and goals are shared.
- **Respond:** Stay proactive, not reactive, in maintaining engagement.
- **Prioritize:** Know where to invest your time and energy for maximum impact.
- **Evaluate:** Continuously assess and refine your relationships over time.

In Part II, you'll learn how this system can help you *move from reactive to strategic* in how you manage relationships—so you're no longer at the mercy of circumstances but shaping them to your advantage.

Once you've read and applied the lessons from Parts I and II, you'll have the confidence to:

- Identify which relationships truly move the needle—and which ones drain your time.
- Cultivate trust and alignment without losing yourself.
- Navigate conflict and power dynamics with board members, investors, and stakeholders.
- Create a culture of engagement and accountability within your leadership team.
- Manage collaborators, consultants, and partners with precision and respect.
- Strengthen your public reputation and community influence.
- Sustain your personal energy and presence as a leader.

When you integrate the six arenas with the CARPE framework, you'll move from a reactive operator to a *relational strategist*.

This book won't waste your time with vague platitudes about "networking" or "being a people person." This is a playbook for CEOs—a practical, actionable guide for using relationships to drive results.

WHO I AM AND WHY I WROTE THIS BOOK

I've spent more than thirty years in business—twenty-five of them as a CEO. I've launched startups, built teams, sold companies, and served on the boards of banks, fintech firms, private and public companies, US government agencies, and nonprofits.

I founded Apollo Bank during one of the most chaotic moments in financial history—the great financial crisis—when the entire banking system was collapsing and fear ruled the market. We built that company from the ground up, not because we had the most capital or the best timing, but because we had the strongest relationships.

Those relationships—investors, regulators, employees, clients, and community leaders—carried us through uncertainty. And they became the foundation for a culture that thrived long after the storm passed.

I've since served as chairman of the Inter-American Foundation, an independent US government agency, after being nominated by the president of the United States and confirmed by the US Senate. I've also served on the boards of Seacoast Bank, the Federal Home Loan Bank of Atlanta, and several private companies. I have been a member of the EO and YPO communities for over twenty years and learned from countless entrepreneurs and CEOs who deal with the challenges of leadership every day.

Today, I coach CEOs and founders who are navigating the same pressures I once faced: managing growth, aligning teams, negotiating with partners, and balancing personal well-being with professional demands.

And the pattern I see in every great leader I work with—the ones who scale sustainably and lead with purpose—is that they've mastered the relational game.

That's what this book is about. It's a field manual for relational leadership: how to see your company as a network of living relationships, and how to lead that network with empathy, clarity, and strength.

WHAT THIS BOOK IS—AND WHAT IT'S NOT

This is *not* a book about being nice to people and hoping things work out.

This is a book about strategic relationships—about understanding how power, influence, and trust shape the world you operate in and how to manage those dynamics with precision.

If you're looking for a generic leadership book that tells you to "be a better listener," this isn't it.

If you want a real, proven system for mastering relationships at the highest levels of business, you're in the right place.

Now that you understand *why* relationships are the real currency of leadership, the next step is to learn *who* you need to focus on.

Let's get to work.

PART I

THE SIX RELATIONSHIPS

<u>Chapter 1</u>

THE BOSSES

Everyone has a boss.

George Steinbrenner was the most powerful owner in professional sports. Under his stewardship, the New York Yankees won seven World Series championships and eleven American League championships. He restored the glory of the marquee franchise and built a sports and media empire. He led an investment group that purchased the team in 1973 for $8.8 million—today the franchise is estimated to be worth more than $8 billion. He set the standard for how Major League Baseball (MLB) franchises could maximize TV rights deals and dramatically increased the value of teams across the league.

Steinbrenner's autocratic and demanding management style earned him the nickname "The Boss," and he loved it. He played it up in Miller Lite commercials, hosted *Saturday Night Live*, and was famous for impromptu press conferences in his hotel suite or outside Yankee Stadium. Though not the sole owner, his minority partners were silent and deferential. They didn't have influence—they had season tickets. His fellow owners respected him because his success raised the tide for everyone.

But even the Boss had a boss.

In 1990, MLB Commissioner Fay Vincent banned Steinbrenner from baseball. Vincent, a polished, Ivy League–educated former securities lawyer, had no prior sports experience. But when Steinbrenner paid a gambler $40,000 to dig up dirt on Yankees outfielder Dave Winfield—with whom he was in a legal dispute—Vincent ruled that the act was unethical and detrimental to the integrity of the game. He issued a lifetime ban, later reduced to two years. For all Steinbrenner's bravado, he found out the hard way: There's always someone you can't fire.

Whether you lead a Fortune 500 company or a family-run firm, you have a boss. This chapter explores who those bosses are, why they matter, and how your relationship with them can make or break your career.

WHAT MAKES A BOSS A BOSS?

The obvious definition of a boss is anyone above you on the org chart. They hired you. They can fire you. They approve your compensation and conduct your performance review. If they can make your life miserable or force you to quit, they're a boss—even if you have the corner office.

If you're the CEO, your bosses might include a chairman, the board of directors, a majority owner, or institutional investors. If you're in a regulated industry, your regulator is your boss. Sometimes your boss isn't even in the company—it might be someone with influence over your board, like a friend, advisor, or family member who whispers in the right ear.

Jamie Dimon, widely respected as one of the most successful modern CEOs, is a case in point. Before leading JPMorgan Chase, he was the heir apparent at Citigroup under his mentor Sandy Weill. But after a series of personal and political conflicts—including issues with Weill's daughter, a Citigroup executive—Dimon was fired. He wasn't outperformed; he was outmaneuvered.

Your boss isn't always the person with the title. Sometimes, it's the person who controls the person with the title.

Bosses come in many forms, but I group them into four primary categories:

1. The Ultimate Boss
2. Board Members and Partners
3. Shareholders and Minority Partners
4. Regulators

Let's look at each one.

THE ULTIMATE BOSS

General Douglas MacArthur was one of the most decorated military leaders in US history. His leadership in the Pacific during World War II and postwar Japan earned him national hero status. But in 1951, despite his stature, he was fired by President Harry Truman during the Korean War.

Why? MacArthur defied orders, pushed for escalating conflict with China, and showed open disrespect toward civilian leadership. The final straw came when MacArthur showed up late to a meeting with Truman at Wake Island—deliberately. He made the president wait, offered no apology, and sat with a casual disregard for decorum.

Truman saw this not just as a policy dispute, but a personal challenge to the authority of the presidency. So he made a statement: No one is above the chain of command.

Robert Greene, in *The 48 Laws of Power*, calls this Law 1: Never Outshine the Master. "Always make those above you feel comfortably superior. In your desire to impress them, do not go too far."

Your Ultimate Boss is the person who holds the final authority. If you're a founder or sole owner, this might not apply. But for most leaders, there is someone whose approval you must earn and maintain.

To manage this relationship well:

- **Get clear.** Understand their goals, fears, and definitions of success. Ask them directly, if appropriate: "What does success look like to you? What keeps you up at night?" If they're not forthcoming, reverse-engineer their priorities based on what they track, question, or reward. Talk to their assistant or trusted inner circle. Review speeches or interviews if they're public-facing. Be a student of how they think.

- **Build a playbook.** Create an "Owner's Manual" based on how they operate. How do they like to receive updates—email, memo, phone call, face-to-face? Do they like lots of detail or just the headline? What are their pet peeves? What language or metrics resonate with them? Keep notes. Adjust your style to theirs, not the other way around.

- **Make an impression, then leave.** Respect their time. Open with the headline, not the buildup. Use bullet points, not long-winded explanations. If you're asked for thirty minutes, plan to deliver in twenty. Exceed expectations and exit early—it builds trust and shows confidence.

- **Act, don't argue.** As Greene puts it, win through actions, not arguments. When you disagree, don't escalate into debate. Instead, say, "Let me show you," and prove your point through results. Execution earns credibility faster than words ever will.

Mastering this relationship requires humility and discipline, but it also builds the foundation for every other power dynamic you'll face. Once you learn how to manage "up"—to anticipate the needs of the person with ultimate authority—you can apply the same principles to groups of power. Boards, investors, and partners may not sit in the same chair, but they hold similar influence over your future. The same rules apply: clarity, respect, and results over rhetoric.

BOARD MEMBERS AND PARTNERS

A CEO who doesn't answer to one person often answers to many: a board or group of partners. These individuals may not run the company, but they can override decisions, shape strategy, or end your tenure.

Take Alan Mulally's time at Ford. When he stepped in as CEO in 2006, the company was in dire straits. Ford had lost billions, mortgaged nearly all its assets—including its iconic blue oval logo—and was staring down the barrel of the Great Recession. Confidence was low among investors, employees, and board members alike. Many wondered whether the company could survive without a government bailout.

Mulally brought a clear, focused strategy: the "One Ford" plan. He aimed to unify Ford's global operations, streamline product development, and focus on building vehicles customers actually wanted. But bold plans require board support—and that's where Mulally excelled. He didn't try to dazzle the board with charisma or sell them a vision full of fluff. Instead, he invited them into the process.

Every Thursday morning, Mulally ran "Business Plan Review" meetings that were rigorous, consistent, and transparent. No sugarcoating. Executives were expected to present data, openly admit setbacks, and identify clear next steps. This culture of candor trickled up to the board. Mulally didn't posture—he reported. He laid out problems, owned them, and showed a plan to fix them. Over time, this built tremendous trust.

By keeping the board informed—not just when things were good but especially when they weren't—Mulally earned their confidence. When the time came to make tough calls, like mortgaging the company's assets or refusing a government bailout, the board backed him. He made them feel like insiders, not outsiders. And in return, they gave him room to lead.

Boards want three things:

- **Protection.** Don't expose them to legal, financial, or reputational risk. Make sure internal controls are robust, your leadership team is held accountable, and no one is putting the company—or the board—in legal jeopardy.
- **Clarity.** Communicate issues early and plainly. Don't let them read about a problem in the press or discover a surprise in a quarterly update. Get out ahead of bad news, and own the narrative.
- **Confidence.** They need to trust your judgment and follow-through. That means consistent performance, transparency, and a clear command of the facts when you walk into the room.

As the CEO, you are not powerless when dealing with board members; you have the ability to set expectations with your board:

- **Come prepared.** No freeloaders. Make sure each board member receives clear agendas, prereads, and financial summaries in advance—and let them know you expect them to engage with that material.
- **No end runs.** They don't manage the business—you do. Board members who bypass the CEO and engage with staff or executives directly are crossing the line. Shut that down immediately.
- **No surprises.** Transparency beats theater. If something goes wrong, your board should hear it from you first. It builds credibility and creates space for support.
- **What's said in the room stays in the room.** Encourage honest discussion and protect it with confidentiality. Open dialogue dies when private comments are leaked.

Troublesome board members? Make them do the work. Assign follow-ups. Ask them to back up their comments with research, contacts, or a written plan. If they say, "I know someone who can fix this," respond with, "Great—can you set up an introduction by Friday?" If they fail to follow through, they'll expose their own lack of seriousness without you having to say a word.

And remember: Sometimes, all a board member wants is to be heard. Take the note, thank them for their input, then do what's best. I call this the "Larry Sanders Model," inspired by the classic HBO satire *The Larry Sanders Show*. In the show, studio executives constantly meddle with the creative direction, offering unwanted feedback. Rip Torn's character, the savvy producer, would nod politely, responding with, "Great note. We'll think about it," and then promptly ignore it. Sometimes, that's the play. You don't have to take every piece of advice—just make people feel like they were heard.

SHAREHOLDERS AND MINORITY PARTNERS

Being entrusted with shareholders' capital is not a right—it's a privilege that a CEO must earn and continually reearn. You earn that right by being transparent, accountable, and relentlessly focused on performance. Whether your shareholder base is made up of institutional investors, longtime family members, or just you—if you're a 100 percent owner—the discipline remains the same: Act in the best interest of the shareholders. That means making decisions based on long-term value creation, not short-term convenience or personal comfort. If you can't or won't do that, then the right thing to do is give the money back. A true CEO always thinks like a shareholder—because in the end, that's who you work for.

Even if you are the largest—or only—shareholder, you need to behave as though you're managing someone else's money. This is how great CEOs build trust and avoid entitlement. Fragmented shareholder bases, passive investors, or minority partners may not be vocal, but that doesn't make them irrelevant. Silent shareholders still have rights and expectations. As CEO, your fiduciary obligation is to safeguard and grow their investment.

To manage shareholder relationships well, you need more than just good financials—you need rhythm and transparency:

- **Communicate consistently.** Send out investor updates, even if it feels like no one's reading them. Hold regular shareholder meetings. Don't go quiet when things get hard—that's when shareholders most need to hear from you.
- **Understand your governance and risk exposure.** Sit down with your lawyer and map out your obligations. Can minority shareholders block a sale? Can they force a distribution? Do they have a vote in setting executive pay? Don't wait until you're mid-crisis to find out what they can and can't do.
- **Document everything.** Keep formal records of capital calls, agreements, votes, and meeting minutes. Good documentation keeps relationships from turning personal during difficult decisions.

All of the above becomes even more important—and more complicated—when shareholders are family members. Many CEOs I talk to list this as their number one source of pain. Why? Because emotions, expectations, and history often cloud business judgment.

It's not unusual to encounter the lazy uncle, the entitled in-law, or the distant cousin who wants influence without contribution. And these personalities can derail not just meetings, but your sanity. Family shareholders may not understand the business, but they still feel ownership—sometimes literally. That dynamic makes clear rules and outside structure absolutely essential.

The best CEOs take the ambiguity out of family–shareholder relationships. Here are a few proven ways to do that:

- **Create a buy–sell agreement.** This sets rules around who can sell their shares, to whom, at what price, and under what conditions.
- **Establish employment policies.** If family members want to work in the business, make sure the bar is high. One of my longtime clients, who runs a one-hundred-year-old family business in South Florida, created a formal family constitution. It states that:
  - You must have a college degree.
  - You must work outside the business for at least two years.

- If you want a management role, you must earn an advanced degree.
  - You must work in the business for five years before being considered for management.
  - You must gain experience in at least two divisions before promotion to an executive position.
- **Bring in a third-party advisor.** An outside voice—someone who understands family business dynamics—can be the buffer between logic and emotion. Often, they can say what the CEO can't.

At the end of the day, the goal is to remove ambiguity. Set the terms for how shareholders—especially family—interact with the business. If someone can't accept those terms, it may be best to pay them out and move on. Sometimes, buying Uncle Jimmy's peace and quiet is the best ROI you'll ever get.

REGULATORS

We're taught there are three branches of government—but in business, there's a fourth: the administrative agencies. Over the past few decades, state and federal regulators have gained more influence over a CEO's fate than any mayor, governor, or even president. One mid-level bureaucrat can block a license, stall an acquisition, or derail an expansion. You can't fire them, but they can shut you down.

Consider Dick Fuld, CEO of Lehman Brothers. In 2008, he ran one of Wall Street's powerhouses—until three unelected officials decided not to bail him out during the financial crisis. Their decision, driven as much by politics as by policy, ended his career overnight.

Now contrast that with Mary Barra at General Motors in 2014. She inherited a deadly ignition-switch crisis, took ownership, met with victims' families, launched reforms, and went straight to Congress before regulators forced the issue. By showing accountability early, she built credibility, kept regulators onside, and preserved GM's reputation.

Two CEOs, two very different outcomes: Fuld got stonewalled; Barra got proactive. Regulators have the power to decide your fate—so don't wait until a crisis to meet them.

Five ways to get ahead of regulators:

- Build relationships early—before you need a favor.
- Retain counsel who know your industry and its watchdogs.
- Keep communication open, even when nothing's wrong.
- Show visible accountability when mistakes happen.
- Accept that you can't control their decisions—but you can influence their perception of you.

You don't set the rules. But you can decide how ready you are when they're enforced.

Remember, as a CEO, you don't get to keep your job just by avoiding mistakes. You keep it by mastering the relationships that matter—starting with your bosses. But that's only part of the equation. Because while bosses may control your job security, it's *your team* that will determine your legacy. In the next chapter, we'll look at how to build trust, alignment, and high performance with the people who follow your lead.

QUICK RELATIONSHIP AUDIT

Before you turn the page, take five minutes and ask yourself:

- Who *technically* has the power to remove me?
- Who *informally* influences that decision?
- When's the last time I checked in—without needing something?
- Do I know what matters most to them right now?
- Do I know their "Owner's Manual"? (Preferred style, quirks, pet peeves?)

If you don't know the answers, you don't really know your boss.

KEY TAKEAWAYS

- **Even the boss has a boss.** Map real power—not just titles—and understand you truly influences outcomes, decisions, and your future.
- **Manage up with precision.** Speak their language, anticipate their priorities, and prove your credibility through consistent execution.
- **Family shareholders need rules.** Clarity beats drama because defined expectations protect both relationships and the business from emotional decision-making.
- **Board confidence, not theatrics.** Be early, be honest, and be ready so trust is built through transparency.
- **Regulators aren't fair.** Build trust before you need it by showing respect, consistency, and outreach long before pressure appears.

Chapter 2

THE TEAM

Jim Harbaugh climbed the stage drenched in sweat and Gatorade, trophy in hand. He didn't give a speech. He grinned, looked at his players, and barked, "Who's got it better than us?"

"*Nobody!*" the Michigan Wolverines roared back.

The 2023 season was one for the history books—undefeated, a national championship, and a program that looked unstoppable. Yet it began with a crisis: Three games in, Harbaugh wasn't even allowed on the sidelines—benched by his own self-imposed suspension while the NCAA poked around alleged recruiting violations. For many teams, that would have been a season-derailing distraction. For Michigan, it was a test they passed with ease, going 3–0 without their head coach on the sidelines.

That resilience came from more than talent. Harbaugh had built a web of strong relationships up and down the organization—relationships based on trust, empowerment, and shared purpose. His coordinators, Sherrone Moore and Jesse Minter, did more than fill in; they led with confidence because Harbaugh had invested in them for years, giving them ownership and influence long before the crisis hit.

The same was true on the field. Leaders like quarterback J.J. McCarthy and running back Blake Corum kept the team accountable and focused, proving that Michigan's culture was bigger than any one person. Harbaugh's relational leadership meant everyone knew their role, felt valued, and was prepared to lead when called upon.

That's the kind of team every CEO should want—deep, trusted, and resilient. In business, as in football, winning isn't just about schemes or resources—it's about the people you choose, the bonds you build, and the culture you nurture so the organization thrives, even when you're not in the room. In the pages ahead, we'll explore how to assemble that kind of core leadership group, keep connections strong across your company, and harness both your "superstars" and your "glue guys" to shape lasting performance and culture.

Let's start with the foundational engine behind it all: building a *People Machine*.

THE PEOPLE MACHINE

The best CEOs I've worked with all share one core strength: They know how to build a team—and they're unapologetic about it. They don't wait around for human resources (HR) to fix things. They take ownership. They choose the right people, remove the wrong ones, and create a system that gets stronger over time. That system is what I call the People Machine.

A People Machine is the engine of your business. It doesn't just hire people and plug them in. It's a living, breathing system that continuously identifies top candidates, selects the right ones through a rigorous process, and brings them into the company with clarity and purpose. It trains them, coaches them, holds them accountable, and keeps the best people growing and engaged. It also knows when to reassess and when to say goodbye. When this machine is working well, your business becomes unstoppable. When it's broken, it doesn't matter how good your product or strategy is—things will grind to a halt. But at its core, the People Machine is not about processes—it's about relationships. Every hire, every promotion, every coaching moment is a chance to build trust and shape culture. Systems don't create results—people do, through their relationships with each other and with you.

And make no mistake: Building this machine is your job. Not HR's. Not your COO's. Yours. As CEO, you have to make building a People Machine one of your company's core priorities. Talk about it often. Tie it to your strategy. Celebrate it publicly. This isn't just a good business practice—it's how great companies are built.

That means recruiting champions who believe in this idea and can drive it forward. Your head of HR is important, but they can't do it alone. Your department heads need to be talent builders, not just task executors. They need to see hiring, onboarding, coaching, and performance management as central to their role—not a side job they delegate away. You need to make it clear that people who build great teams will be promoted and rewarded, and those who don't won't last.

You also need to confront the sacred cows. Every organization has them—people who were there at the beginning, or who are technically brilliant but culturally toxic. Maybe they hold a lot of institutional knowledge or they're tied to someone important. But if they're dragging your team down, they have to go. One of the fastest ways to kill the momentum of a People Machine is to let everyone see that mediocrity is tolerated. If you want people to believe you're serious, make one hard call—and let people see it.

Most importantly, you have to invest in this process and keep reinforcing it. Don't just talk about it once in a speech and assume it'll happen. Put in the work to build a structured, repeatable system. If you're looking for a place to start, the Topgrading method and the book *Who* by Geoff Smart are excellent resources. But don't stop at hiring—make sure onboarding is meaningful, performance reviews are taken seriously, and people are constantly being developed. And even when things are going well, keep the machine oiled. The moment you start coasting, it starts breaking down.

Ed Catmull, co-founder of Pixar, said it best: "If you give a good idea to a mediocre team, they'll screw it up. If you give a mediocre idea to a brilliant team, they'll either fix it or throw it out and come up with something better." That's the magic of the People Machine. It's not just about talent—it's about the system that turns talent into results. And it's your job to build it.

The commitment to building a People Machine starts with the CEO, but it is carried out through the senior leadership team, who directly reports to the leader who provides counsel and oversees the business and makes things happen through their own direct reports. How the CEO manages the relationship with the senior leadership team collectively and the members individually will determine how decisions are made throughout the organization, and we will cover this next.

Let's explore the dynamics with the *senior leadership team* now.

THE SENIOR LEADERSHIP TEAM

Your company's success starts with your senior leadership team. They set the standard.

Marc Andreessen, the legendary creator of the web browser and founder of Andreessen Horowitz, has said that his "big pivot" was moving from investing based on ideas and concepts to focusing on people, teams, and relationships. He also discovered that the best startups in tech weren't necessarily about the tech but about the people and the team. Andreessen says that venture capital needs to bet on people, because the business changes and even if the idea is good, the people need to execute.

The senior leadership team will be different in each organization, but it will usually consist of the top three to six direct reports to the CEO. For large organizations, a senior leadership team may consist of twelve people, but beyond that it's really not the "senior" leadership team and it's more of a management team. What we are talking about is the core team that serve as the key confidantes and decision-makers in the company. The members of the team usually consist of the chief financial officer (CFO), chief operations officer (COO), the head of sales/revenue, and the person who heads up product and service. The senior leadership, if the group is larger, will also include the head of human resources, the head of information technology, and a person involved in risk management. But once you go beyond eight people, it's probably too many (see the Jeff Bezos/Amazon two pizza rule: A meeting should only involve as many people as can be fed with two pizzas).

The CEO needs to first see this group as one entity and a relationship they need to manage. The health of the team, not just the individuals, is critical. When we look at the most successful teams, what comes to mind are the great sports team dynasties, the Navy SEALS, and the Apollo team of NASA. The traits they had in common were:

- Transparency
- Clear definition of winning
- Great skill of the individuals
- Accountability
- Membership based purely on merit
- Trust

We can look to Google for another great example. I'm not talking about typing this into your search browser but by looking at the exhaustive study the company conducted on the topic called Project Aristotle. Google's Project Aristotle found that the most important factor in a great team is *psychological safety*, where team members feel safe to take risks and express themselves without fear of judgment. Other key elements include *dependability, clear structure and goals, meaningful work*, and a shared belief that the work has impact. These findings emphasize that how a team interacts is more critical than who is on the team.

Even the best leadership team can drift without rhythm. Transparency, trust, and skill create potential, but cadence is what drives performance. The CEO's job isn't just to assemble a great team; it's to keep that team connected, aligned, and focused through deliberate, recurring conversations. That means building a system of interaction—*Priorities Meetings*, one-on-ones, and check-ins—that make relationships stronger and decisions sharper. Consistency in communication is what transforms a group of talented individuals into a true leadership team.

THE PRIORITIES MEETING

If you want your leadership team aligned, focused, and accountable, don't wait for a quarterly off-site or an annual strategy session. You need rhythm. You need a weekly drumbeat. That's what the Priorities Meeting is for.

This isn't just another "staff meeting." It's the most important meeting on your calendar. When run well, it becomes the cultural heartbeat of your company.

Set the Rhythm

Hold it the same day, same time, every week. Start on time. End on time. No one's too busy. No one's too important to skip. This consistency builds discipline and signals that execution matters. Use a shared document (I like OneNote or Google Docs) for the agenda, key metrics, and takeaways—keep everything centralized and visible.

Open with Good News

Start with a quick round of personal good news—something no one in the room already knows. A kid's soccer win, a trip they're planning, an anniversary, anything. This simple ritual does two things: It humanizes the team, and it gives you, the CEO, a quick read on everyone's energy and engagement.

Review the Scoreboard

Next, move to the numbers. The metrics that matter this week. Everyone should review them ahead of time—this is not the time for long explanations or spinning stories. If something's off, flag it. If something needs deeper discussion, drop it into the "parking lot" and come back to it. Don't get bogged down here—this is a pulse check, not a postmortem.

Collective Intelligence

This is the heart of the meeting. Ask: Where are we stuck? What needs a group solution? What are you hearing that we should all know? The CEO should share what's on their mind too—vision updates, concerns, or directional shifts. But this is a dialogue, not a monologue. The goal is real-time collaboration, not just reporting out.

Check the Pulse: Customers and Employees

Before you wrap, go around the room and ask: What are you hearing from customers? From employees? If nobody brings anything, that's a red flag. Your senior leaders should have a pulse on the front lines. If they don't, they're flying blind—and so are you.

Close with Takeaways

Finish strong. Recap the key decisions, next steps, and who owns what. Then ask each team member to share their "one big takeaway" from the meeting. It keeps everyone engaged and surfaces any gaps in understanding before you leave the room.

Meetings are often seen as a necessary evil, but when they're done right, they become a relationship-strengthening ritual. It's how you build rhythm, trust, and cohesion across the leadership team. It creates momentum. It keeps priorities clear. It reinforces culture. It gives your team a rhythm they can trust.

As CEO, your job is not just to attend—*it's to lead the meeting.* Set the tone. Be clear on what matters most. And show up ready to work.

The rhythm of the senior leadership teams is how you build the relationship with the team, but how you build relationships with each member of the senior leadership team is through *One-on-One* meetings with each individual of the team.

Let's explore those next.

ONE-ON-ONES

If you want to build trust with your team, you need to make time for One-on-One meetings. Not performance reviews. Not hallway chats. I mean real, focused conversations that happen on a regular rhythm. The kind that help you understand your people—and let them understand you.

Make It a Habit

The frequency depends on the person and the situation, but there's no excuse for skipping these. Quarterly is the bare minimum. Monthly is better. And for your most critical lieutenants—the ones managing major projects or leading big initiatives—weekly isn't overkill. Don't wait for a problem to arise. These meetings should be proactive, not reactive.

Set the Tone

This is not a therapy session. Still, this is where the relationship gets built. People don't give their best to leaders they don't know or trust. These meetings are your most direct opportunity to show you care about the person behind the role. You control the tone and the agenda. You can be warm, even personal—but don't lose sight of why you're there. Every One-on-One should have structure. That doesn't mean a script, but it does mean a clear flow: check in, align on goals, address priorities, and make decisions. Let them bring their issues to the table, but bring your own too.

Start Human

Kick things off with a genuine check-in. How's life outside of work? Anything new going on? This isn't small talk—it's relationship-building. You want your people to feel seen. You're not just their boss; you're their partner in this thing.

Review the Scoreboard

What are they accountable for? Are the numbers where they should be? This isn't about catching them off guard—it's about alignment. You want to see if you're looking at the same problems through the same lens. If you're not, that's the first problem to solve.

Open the Table

Ask what they need from you. What's slowing them down? Where are they stuck? What do they see that you don't? This is their chance to surface issues, float ideas, or ask for support. But don't just listen— coach them. Push their thinking. Challenge their assumptions. Help them grow.

Share What's on Your Mind

Now it's your turn. What do they need to hear from you? Is there feedback you've been sitting on? A pattern you've noticed? A shift in focus they need to make? Speak clearly, directly, and with purpose. This is where leadership happens.

Check Their Team

Before you close, zoom out. How's their team doing? Who's crushing it? Who's on the edge? What dynamics are brewing below the surface? Your executives are your window into the broader organization—and how they talk about their people tells you a lot about how they're leading.

Lock In the Takeaways

Don't let the conversation end in the air. Summarize what was discussed. Recap action items. Be clear on what's expected before the next One-on-One. And then follow up. The most powerful form of accountability is consistency.

If you do this well—regularly, thoughtfully, and with intention—One-on-Ones become one of the most valuable leadership tools you have. They're not just meetings. They're how you shape culture, build loyalty, and stay connected to what's really happening in your company.

There is no one way to manage individuals, and every CEO will have to find their way with the team they have.

Every situation is different. You could be operating a business in a mature industry with limited new growth opportunities and single-digit growth is considered a success. You may be in a turnaround situation, where you are focused not so much on "winning" but on surviving. Other situations require a different skillset. Startups come to mind. Some organizations may be in an "all in" situation. If that's the case, you need to hire an "all in" core team. Elon Musk tackles problems where a 10x or even a 100x improvement is needed, which is most likely not your situation.

As your organization grows, it is impossible to have a direct relationship with all of your employees, even some very critical ones, so you have to work through your senior leadership team in order to have a pulse on your people. If you aren't working through your senior leadership team, you may prescribe the wrong medicine.

A great example comes from NBA Head Coach Doc Rivers, who has seen countless players struggle through slumps. He points out that a bad performance doesn't necessarily mean the player isn't talented. That's where his assistant coaches come in—they help him understand what's really happening. For instance, one coach might say, "Man, this guy is in the gym every day, taking one thousand shots and pushing himself hard. He's too tight." Another might point out a player who's coasting and not putting in the effort. If Rivers were to tell the over-worked player to push harder, he'd only make things worse. Likewise, if he advised the slacker to relax, he'd be reinforcing bad habits.

The takeaway? Leaders need to rely on their senior team to stay informed about what's happening with those a level or two below them. Understanding the full picture is key to making the right calls.

This is like the "good news" feature in your weekly priorities meetings. The primary reason you do this is to start the meeting on a positive note and to prime the meeting. But you also want to hear about the team members and see them as whole individuals. Another reason you want to do this is because you want to see which members of your leadership team are truly engaged with the employee base—who has a pulse on what is going on in the organization and what that pulse tells you about your company's health.

This leads us to your broader *employee base*, the ones you can't interact with every day but are still critical for you to develop a relationship in a different way.

YOUR EMPLOYEE BASE

"I don't run racing cars; I run people that run racing cars."

This is not what you'd expect to hear from the billionaire CEO and co-owner of the Mercedes-AMG PETRONAS F1 Team, Toto Wolff. Under Wolff's leadership, Mercedes-Benz's F1 racing team has won an unprecedented eight team championships. He attributes the team's success not just to world champion driver Lewis Hamilton or the financial backing of the German automotive powerhouse. Instead, he credits the culture he has worked hard to cultivate and the high standard for excellence he sets for all employees—not just his drivers or engineers. As he put it, "It is not necessarily the best individuals that win races, but the team that best works together."

When he took over the Mercedes program, he found that the organization's employees were not aligned. He believes setting the right tone and attitude for employees starts with the smallest details— because everything matters.

On his first day at work, he noticed empty coffee cups and old magazines cluttering the reception area. He immediately scolded everyone, saying this was unacceptable for a group pursuing greatness. First impressions matter, he told them, and attention to detail sets the standard to whomever walks through the front door.

On his first race day, he saw that the bathrooms in the paddocks, used by guests and supporters, were filthy after the first hour. The next week, he didn't just assign the problem to the cleaning crew. Instead, he found some rubber gloves and a pail, and instructed his entire staff on how to clean the bathrooms—because everything represented the Mercedes-Benz brand, and no one was above maintaining excellence.

As he puts it: "People interested in F1 always ask us about the car, but they should be asking about the organization, because that is what is special."

When you run an organization as big as Toto Wolff's (thousands of employees across the globe), you can't talk to every employee, but you can set an example that carries a message long after you leave the room.

Let's explore some tools every leader needs to use to build relationships with their employee base.

COMMUNICATION

Your people aren't just craving information—they're craving context. As Simon Sinek points out, "More information is always better than less. When people know the reason things are happening, even if it's bad news, they can adjust their expectations and react accordingly. Keeping people in the dark only serves to stir negative emotions."

CEOs often assume people know the "why" behind decisions, but they don't. That's your job. The CEO's voice is the story. And the story is what people remember. As the leader you need to constantly communicate with your broad base of employees. Chances are, the CEO doesn't go home and talk about individual employees with their families. If the leader does "bring their work home" they are probably talking about a client or a competitor or a lawsuit, not talking about Sally in accounting who got engaged or Sanjay who is going on a camping trip this weekend. But your employees are talking about you. They think about you and talk about you—you are an important person in their life. So you should care a little about what they are saying. It's a responsibility, an opportunity, and also a risk.

Here are some of my tips for improving your communications with employees.

You Are the Storyteller in Chief

Storytelling is one of the greatest tools a leader can use to communicate. The storyteller sets the vision, values, and agenda of what's to come. Find stories that tie back and enforce your company's core values. Tell the stories of the company's challenges and how they overcame them; tell the stories of the employees who rose above obstacles and worked to help the company succeed.

Management by Walking Around

You walk around the factory or office every day as part of your routine. Make yourself visible and seen. Don't sit at a desk all day and go out to lunch by yourself. Don't let the only time your employees see you is when you get out of your BMW (or whatever car you drive—and yes, your employees have 100 percent noticed what kind of car you drive).

Friday "E"mail

At the company I founded and ran, Apollo Bank, I would send out a Friday "E"mail (My name is Eddy, I was sending an email, it was my message—get it?). Looking back, it was one of the most effective things I did. It connected me to the employees, made me real, and gave them things to talk about. It reinforced our core values through storytelling. I'd get our people to think about their role in the community (ideas for things to do over the weekend, events happening around town, ways to volunteer). I'd highlight stories at the company that most employees didn't know and I'd search for opportunities to reinforce priorities and core values. This was not a newsletter! I'd reinforce that over and over—the email wasn't a place for baby announcements or award recognition. I made it specific as to what was going on in my head and how it might apply to them and the future of our company. I'd talk about the importance of voting in local elections, encourage reading, invited all employees to join a book club I moderated, mentioned what movies I was watching. I wanted people to be *interested and interesting.* We were in a client-service business and I wanted our employees to have interesting things to talk about with our clients. The Friday "E"mails had a lasting impact because I kept them authentic.

Town Halls

A town hall meeting hearkens back to the days when people lived in small communities and neighbors would meet up in the center of town to discuss what was going on in the community. I am a proponent of bringing all your employees together a few times a year. You don't have to do this physically anymore; with Zoom and video conferences, it has become so much easier.

I don't think the meetings should be long or convey too much information. The leader should talk, gather everyone together, and also have the opportunity to listen to employees. I recommend not overcomplicating the agenda. Don't read from a PowerPoint unless it's absolutely necessary, and if it is, keep it simple and use easy-to-understand graphics. As CEO, you are the chief reminding officer. Just keep reinforcing what is important: priorities and core values. People want to have a forum to hear from their leader and ask questions—if they desire. Town hall meetings are not the venue for awards ceremonies, but you can and should call out specific individuals for specific accomplishments and behaviors you want to highlight within the organization.

Company Picnics

Big get-togethers where your employees are all in one place and bring their families to celebrate being a part of the company is a super powerful tool to build a relationship with your employees. The CEO may feel like a presidential candidate at the Iowa State Fair, trying to guess the weight of a hog or eating the world's largest funnel cake, as they go around saying hello to everyone and their families, but this is important to employees. They will remember this forever. Kids get to see their parent's coworkers and gain a greater appreciation for the work they do everyday. Coworkers get to see each other in regular weekend attire, you meet people and you find stuff out—*Oh, I didn't know Karen's kid uses a wheelchair,* or that *Jimmy's mother-in-law lives with them* or that *Maria met her spouse while they were both serving in the military in the Philippines (who knew?!).* You don't have to have a giant blowout party; it's all about bringing people together to celebrate. Not sure what to do for your next corporate picnic? Find the best BBQ spot in town and have them bring a mobile smoker and an extra pitmaster who will grill ribs and chicken for you all day.

Cascading Conversations

You may find that your organization is too large and widespread or that your schedule is too constrained, but that doesn't mean you don't keep trying to connect with all your employees. One way to make sure they are being "touched" is by cascading your conversations—the feedback and message you give to your senior leadership team or maybe your "two down" team flows down to other levels. Be clear on messaging and stories, and instruct your team members to have their own contact to say "the boss says."

Videos

Grab your iPhone and shoot a video with a message. You don't have to have a fancy studio with lighting. Keep it real. Share a message for the day. People will more likely watch and share a two-minute video than read your email. But beware of what you say because it will be shared.

There are many ways to communicate with people in your company. We talk about the big gestures—the promotions, the big events, the big wins. But stacking up a lot of little wins over the long haul can have such an impact on the organization and build your culture and build connections and relationships back to your company.

THE LITTLE THINGS

The little things matter.

Here are some simple communication strategies that are easy to implement and have a big impact:

Handwritten Notes and Birthday Cards

Sending handwritten notes and birthday cards is a lost art but it hasn't lost its power. In fact, because so little personal mail goes out, sending someone a card and having them receive it via mail is an incredibly touching and impactful gesture. Each year, I would send each of my employees a handwritten birthday card for their birthday. It's easier than you think…I'd have HR print out labels of the person's name and address on the first of the month and I'd send out the cards on that date. I had more than one hundred employees so say I had maybe ten per month. It would take a half hour on the first Friday of each month. The payoff was always there. If their grandmother isn't around anymore, chances are your card is the only one they will receive in the mail on their birthday.

Key Employee Dinner

When you are first recruiting a key executive, you may invite them out to dinner and have an extended conversation and meal in order to get to know them and possibly recruit them to join the company. But why only do this for the people you are trying to bring into the organization and not the ones you really want to stay at the company and have an even bigger impact moving forward? I encourage you to make a list of your top twelve most impactful employees and have dinner with them each once a year, one-on-one. A two-hour dinner where you have a deep conversation about work, the future, and their personal lives. Find out what makes them tick. What drives them? Create that glue. Most CEOs are paranoid that one of their best team members is going to walk in one morning and leave for some unknown reason; conversations like the ones you'll have at these dinners will mitigate this disaster.

Target Gift Cards

I remember being a kid, heading to the office supply store with my mom to shop for back-to-school supplies. It was always a struggle. She wanted me to stick to the school's required list, but most of it felt useless to me. And when it came to the pens, the lunchbox, or the clothes? They were never the ones I wanted. It was even harder for my mom because there were five of us kids, and sometimes she'd bring along my cousins, too. For just a few bucks, I would have been thrilled to pick out the right notebook or that cool pen with the erasable ink.

That memory stuck with me. So at Apollo Bank, I started a tradition: Every school-age kid with a parent working at the company got a $25 gift card before the new school year. It didn't matter if they were a biological child, a stepchild, a grandchild, or a kid living in the home—we included as many as possible. Along with the gift card, we sent a note on company stationery that said something like:

"We know back-to-school shopping can be tough. Here's something to help you get ready for the new school year."

It was a small gesture, but it mattered. It showed these kids that Apollo Bank appreciated their parents, that their parents worked somewhere that valued family. I always tried to add a personal touch, scribbling a side note on the letter. If I knew the employee well, I'd include something specific. Otherwise, I'd just write, "Your mom/dad is a rock star."

It became a yearly highlight for the kids. I even included my own and wrote, "Say hi to your Mutha for me,"—a nod to an *SNL* skit with Mark Wahlberg.

After we sold Apollo Bank, one of our former employees told me that when the next school year rolled around, their kids asked, "Hey, where's my letter from Apollo Bank?" That's when I knew the impact this little gesture had on the lives of our team members.

Coffee and Lunch in the Break Room

We can get stuck in our own habits. Maybe you go out to lunch or have client lunches as often as you can. But find the time to go to where your team is and have a coffee in the kitchen or bring your lunch into the break room. What's on TV that they are watching? Who sits with whom? Are the microwaves broken or do you just have one and everyone has to wait? For a couple hundred bucks you can buy ten microwaves and no one has to wait—break the bottleneck; it goes a long way. They may find it more comfortable that you come to them.

Keep It Simple

Use simple language. Don't try to show off. "If you care about being thought credible and intelligent, do not use complex language where simple language will do," writes Nobel Prize–winning economist Daniel Kahneman in *Thinking, Fast and Slow*. He argues that persuasive speakers and writers do everything they can to reduce "cognitive strain."

Office Gossip

Dealing with office gossip is something you have to consider, and you should have a pulse on it. Don't feed it or participate in it, but be aware that it exists in any group of people. The information sheds light on darker sides, rumors, fears, lies, and what is holding people in your organization back (nepotism, rumors of an imminent sale of the company, office romances, favoritism, bureaucracy, bad leaders, bad service by a particular department in the company). Who is willing to share this information with you—who is your mole into this world? It might be someone on your senior leadership team who shares this information with you, or a longtime loyal employee, but it should be someone you can trust who is providing this information for constructive purposes, not to sabotage others. You can't put an end to a rumor if you don't know it exists.

Be Curious

Brian Nichols, chairman and CEO of Starbucks, when he was at Chipotle in meetings with other senior executives, peppered them with questions about their past week: What were their children talking about? What were their kids' friends interested in? In other words, what did Chipotle need to know about pop culture? Having these types of conversations with coworkers is not only incredibly useful to get new information but it shows that you are paying attention and value their opinions.

Ultimately, what matters is that you are connecting with as many people as possible. There are some people, however, who really require your attention because they have an outsized impact on the company's success—these are your *superstars*.

SUPERSTARS

We all have superstars, individuals who are head and shoulders above the rest, who outperform others and truly shine. These are the salespeople who bring in the top clients, exceed the goals by 300 percent, and make more money than everyone else because they produce. These are the individuals who are asked to speak at conferences and have a reputation in your industry.

These are also the individuals who many times request and require a different level of attention and want their own rules. They want their own commission plan or they don't want to comply with the standard corporate travel expense program. They can be demanding and call people out who don't report to them.

You hope that, not only that they continue to perform at a high level, but that they motivate others. True stars make others around them better. Magic Johnson of the LA Lakers was famous for this. He didn't just rack up points—he created true synergy. Players wanted to play with him and be around him.

But do you need superstars to win? Yes. Eric Schmidt, former chairman and CEO of Google, says, "You should hire the divas. You read any management texts and they say, 'Don't hire the divas because they are nothing but a pain in the ass,' and by the way, they are. But the people who are the divas are the ones that will drive the culture of excellence, and they will drive you to the standard of excellence. Steve Jobs was a diva. I mean this in a flattering way. They expect a lot, they drive people hard, they are controversial and they care passionately."

Every successful organization has superstars. This doesn't just apply to professional sports, high-end programmers, or Hollywood actors. You find superstars in every industry and in most winning organizations. CEOs at hospitals have to deal with top surgeons, and at many high schools across the country, school administrators are having to deal with a new crop of superstars at their schools—the big-time coaches who win state championships and rally the alumni back to games and to donate money. You have to treat the head coach of the defending state championship gymnastics team differently than you would the freshman English teacher (no offense, Mr. Holtmann).

One of my clients is a very successful dentist who has built a multimillion-dollar children's dentistry and orthodontics practice. And although Dr. Steven is the head dentist, he is not the practice's superstar; that distinction goes to Sherry. Sherry is the superstar hygienist whom patients request by name. She was Dr. Steven's first employee and she brought in all the business—she grew up in the local neighborhood and raised her family there; she was the home-room mother, was in charge of school fundraisers, and knew all the moms and dads in the area. She was the one who encouraged Dr. Steven to strictly focus on the children's dentistry market. She has her own book of business and a loyal following. But after all these years, Sherry commands a different level of respect around the office even though she is cleaning teeth just like the eight other hygienists. She doesn't want to manage anyone. She no longer works on Fridays and she takes two months off in the summers. She can reject certain patients and makes more than the junior dentist Dr. Stevens recently hired from the University of Florida and much more than any of the other hygienists. But she's worth it because she brings in new clients, has a loyal customer base, and is the heart of the practice's culture.

But how do you treat these people and keep them feeling special while not disrupting the team dynamic? This is a special skill that CEOs need to manage, and how they develop these relationships may determine if the firm succeeds or fails.

WHAT IS A LEADER TO DO WITH SUPERSTARS?

Leading these top performers isn't without its challenges. Their ambition and drive can disrupt team dynamics, while their outsized contributions often require careful recognition and reward. A CEO must strike a delicate balance—fostering their growth and unleashing their potential while ensuring they remain aligned with the broader team and company vision. So, what does it take to lead these exceptional individuals effectively?

Here are some things to keep in mind:

Are they really a superstar? Make sure your company has the right metrics in place and can really assess who is producing at superstar levels. One of my clients was in due diligence on an acquisition target and one of the sticking points was tying up and accommodating the target firm's top salesperson—Marcia. Marcia was the top producer for three years in a row and was putting up better numbers than anyone at my client's company. But it seemed off. As they drilled down into the metrics, Marcia was allowed a level of pricing that no one else was able to offer. She was also allowed to promise different payment terms and service commitments than anyone else—she was basically selling a different product and competing with an advantage over the other sales reps. It's not that she wasn't a good producer, it's that she wasn't a real superstar, and the acquirer made the call that they weren't going to pay her more *and* work off of lower profit margins.

Look at the individuals that you are calling into question and ask whether they are superstars or not—are you winning because of them or they are just putting up big numbers but playing under a different scoring system? The team knows the real answer, and if you get caught treating someone like a superstar who doesn't really fit the mold, your company is going to have a culture problem.

Be careful giving out too much credit. Haralabos Voulgaris, owner of the Spanish soccer team CD Castellon and former consultant to the NBA, leans toward deemphasizing credit to star players: "It's hard when you have a team of twenty-three players; the last thing any one player wants to hear is 'This other guy is the reason we win.'"

Treat them differently. On the show *Mad Men*, one of the lead characters states, "There are rules and there are other rules." Recognize your superstars as individuals. They want to be seen. One way is to allow them leeway, as long as it is within guidelines that don't ruin the culture. A reporter once asked the legendary MLB manager Sparky Anderson if he treated all players the same way and he replied, "Hell no! If Johnny Bench (National Baseball Hall of Fame catcher on the Cincinnati Reds World Championship teams) wants a day off, I say hell yes. If a rookie wants a day off, I say hell no!"

Keep egos in check. In Sebastian Junger's book *Freedom*, he points out that the issue of what to do with "superstars" is something that we've had to deal with in the same way since the dawn of man. Hunter-gatherer communities often went to great lengths to make sure skilled hunters were not held in too high esteem. It's not that these communities were against excellence—in fact they depended on it—but they knew how badly pride and ego can destabilize a group. Junger points out that the counter to this is wealth—if the superstar can contribute enough to the entire organization that the leader is able to distribute the spoils fairly or keep the team within their expectations, things work out.

Pay them what they are worth. Why has LeBron James always been the highest-paid player on his team? Because he's worth it! True superstars provide a disproportionate value to your company, and their performance should be rewarded and celebrated.

How to Talk to Your Superstars

Remember, managing superstars isn't about treating them the same as everyone else. You can't. They often demand more, challenge you more, and perform at levels that make them difficult to replace. But if you get it right, they'll raise the ceiling for your entire company.

The key is to balance three things: *Coach them. Compensate them. Contain them.* Do all three well, and they'll power your business. Miss one, and they might burn it down on the way out.

1. Coach Them

This isn't about weekly check-ins or performance reviews. This is about helping high-performers reach their next level *without letting them forget they're part of a team.*

When you're coaching a superstar, don't just talk about their numbers—talk about their impact. What kind of teammate are they? Are they helping raise the game of those around them? Or are they racking up stats at the expense of everyone else?

As a CEO, when you coach your stars, you want them to hear: *You're great. I believe in you. But part of being great here means making others better too.*

Be careful not to come off as threatened or resentful of their power. Your tone matters. The message should be: *I expect more from you because you're the best.*

You're not managing their ego—you're managing their ambition. Use it. Shape it. Challenge it.

2. Compensate Them

Pay them. Full stop.

There is nothing worse than pretending someone isn't worth what they're clearly worth. If a superstar is delivering disproportionate results, recognize it—with compensation, with flexibility, with access.

That doesn't mean letting them write their own rules. It means recognizing their value and making sure their rewards match the results. If not, someone else will.

3. Contain Them

This is the part most CEOs miss.

When someone is that good, it's tempting to give them free rein. But left unchecked, even the best performers can poison your culture. They can make demands, ignore boundaries, or undermine managers—and no one will say anything because, "Well…she's the rainmaker."

You need to set boundaries. Clear ones.

You can treat people differently. But not unfairly. That's the line.

If a star starts to act like they're above the culture, you have to contain it. Fast. Not with a blowup—but with clarity. Remind them: *You're a huge reason we're successful. But this culture matters. And no one is bigger than the mission.*

You can win with superstars. But only if you lead them—through coaching, compensation, and clear boundaries.

When Superstars Hold You Hostage

At some point an employee will pick a vulnerable moment for the company and say: "Triple my salary or I quit!" You will find yourself in a position you don't want to be in that will test your patience. These types of individuals try to negotiate from a place of strength where they think you have no other option but to agree.

What to do?

- Make sure you really aren't underpaying and you are competitive in the marketplace.
- Avoid this by building a People Machine so you are fine when anyone leaves (having a deep bench of talent).
- Give them what they want to avoid short-term pain but realize they're not a good fit, long term. But take note—they have changed their position from teammate to mercenary. They are not to be considered a key player in your company's long term.
- Be alert to the fact that this really isn't a private event—other people within your organization are watching. Other employees will see how you respond and take note—did you cave; were you fair? And if the individual was being recruited away by a competitor, will they see that you won't respond competitively and that your firm is ripe for further poaching? Keep in mind that many eyes are watching you and it will have rippling impacts on other relationships.

You have to treat your superstars differently, but not everyone is a superstar. There will be key contributors to your organization who are not on your senior leadership team nor might they be the traditional superstars who are big producers or outsized talents compared to others. There will be people in your organization who don't get the accolades and are not getting recruited by competitors, but they are the ones who make your corporate culture, make things happen, and whose loyalty to the company is immeasurable. These are the people who hold it all together—the *glue guys*. In the next section, we will talk about the people who don't regularly get the credit, but who are worth so much to your organization.

GLUE GUYS

In the military, especially in branches like the army or marines, non-commissioned officers (NCOs) are often the backbone of operations. They aren't usually the most decorated or highest-ranking, yet they are responsible for training soldiers, maintaining discipline, and supporting morale. They ensure that orders from higher ranks are carried out effectively and that the troops are prepared for missions. They're not always remembered by name, but their influence on successful missions and troop cohesion is profound. For instance, during World War II, sergeants and corporals were pivotal in ensuring the success of operations across Europe and the Pacific, even though generals like Eisenhower and Patton were the faces of the campaigns.

One of the great examples of this in sports was seen during the Miami Heat's championship runs in 2012 and 2013. Shane Battier was the classic glue guy. He wasn't the main star, with LeBron James, Dwyane Wade, and Chris Bosh getting the limelight, but Battier was known for his gritty defense, high basketball IQ, and ability to hit crucial three-pointers. He provided stability on defense, set an example of selflessness, and was known as a strong communicator on and off the court. His leadership helped foster a team-first mentality that was crucial for their titles.

In government, behind every elected leader are often key staffers and advisors who help shape policies and maintain a sense of cohesion among different departments. For example, Ted Sorensen, speechwriter and advisor to President John F. Kennedy, played an essential yet understated role in shaping the messaging and spirit of JFK's administration. He was especially important during the Cuban Missile Crisis, serving as a key participant in the White House working with the US military and the USSR; although Kennedy was the face, Sorensen's work helped define the tone and direction of much of what was achieved.

The more you look, the more you see the value of these contributors. When you think of the great TV show *Saturday Night Live*, what comes to mind are all the big stars—John Belushi, Will Ferrell, Eddie Murphy, Kristin Wiig. But the show isn't great because it has solo acts doing routines on their own; what has made it magical over fifty years is the ensemble cast, working together to put on a great show. They have longtime writers and players like Kenan Thompson who hasn't really had a breakout character but has been a key contributor for twenty years; and longtime contributors like Tim Meadows, Rachel Dratch, and Fred Armisen who weren't breakout stars on the show but contributed to sketches week after week and brought out the best in the performance of the entire cast.

To a CEO, building relationships with these glue guys is important because they are the carriers of the cultural torch and are fiercely loyal, traits that are especially important during tough times.

HOW DO YOU SPOT GLUE GUYS?

How do you spot glue guys? They are loyalists. They are the people who bring other highly talented individual contributors together and get them to work with others. They break apart fiefdoms. A common characteristic is that they are friends with people in other departments—they are the ones who pull together the baby showers, are on the softball team, and start a fantasy football league to include more people across "collars" and genders. They are willing to play the role and wear the company "jersey" and are proud of it.

Glue guys lead from the middle, from the back, from the side, or from wherever they are. You just don't find them in the front. They are the unsung heroes, outside the limelight.

So what is a CEO to do with the glue guys? Well, they aren't superstars and because of their role you can't lavish them with false praise and fortune. But here are some things that you should be doing:

- **Reward loyalty with loyalty.** True recognition comes when you demonstrate loyalty by investing in their growth, securing their future within the company, and ensuring they feel valued as the cornerstone of your team's success.
- **Do not keep them in the dark.** Even if they aren't at the top of the organizational chart, these individuals should feel like key players. Share your vision with them, involve them in decisions, and let them know they're trusted with the company's future. Their loyalty thrives on feeling valued, not sidelined.
- **Give them tough assignments.** Challenging these loyal team members with high-stakes projects shows that you believe in their abilities and trust them to handle responsibility. It's a clear signal that their contributions matter and that you're committed to their development, even when the road gets tough.
- **Visibility matters.** Let others see you with them one-on-one, so that they have the implied authority and others see that their contributions are appreciated.

Glue guys don't need the world to sing their praises, but they need to know someone sees them. These aren't just employees—they're relationships worth investing in. Loyalty, trust, and shared history are your glue. Treat them that way.

A leader stands on the shoulders of their team. The relationships with all of your employees—especially the key members of your senior leadership team—are what will keep your company performing at the highest levels. Success isn't just about having the right strategy, product, or resources—it's about the people you choose and how you lead them. The best CEOs don't just manage; they build a People Machine—an organization that attracts, develops, and retains top talent while fostering a culture of trust, accountability, and excellence.

From high-performing superstars who drive results to the glue guys who hold everything together, a company thrives when its leaders know how to balance recognition, accountability, and culture. The most effective leaders don't just set the vision—they reinforce it daily through clear communication, strong relationships, and meaningful actions. Whether it's through structured meetings, personal connections, or small but impactful gestures, great leaders ensure their teams feel seen, valued, and motivated. At the end of the day, your company is only as strong as the people who power it.

But there are other important relationships you build with people that don't directly work for you but at times feel very much like your teammates. These are the individuals who work outside your company as advisors and see the world outside your wall while having an invite to come into your company. These are the *collaborators*—your strategic vendors, your lawyers, consultants, advisors, and bankers that provide advice and counsel to you every day and which we'll cover in the next chapter.

QUICK RELATIONSHIP AUDIT

Before you move on, take five minutes and ask yourself:

- Who are the three to five most critical people on my team right now?
- Do I know what matters most to *them*—professionally and personally?
- When's the last time I sat down with each of them, one-on-one, with no distractions?
- Who are the real superstars in my company?

- Who are the glue guys holding this place together—and have I told them?

If you don't know the answers, you're not managing a team—you're managing around one.

Chapter 3

THE COLLABORATORS

"That's thirty minutes away. I'll be there in ten."

Jules and Vincent have lost their cool. A dead body, a bloody car, and an innocent bystander's home are all part of the problem. In Quentin Tarantino's *Pulp Fiction*, chaos reigns when two hitmen, Jules and Vincent, accidentally create a mess. They're out of their depth, out of ideas, and running out of time, so they call their boss, Marsellus Wallace, for help. In a panic, Jules explains the situation to Wallace, to which the boss replies, "You ain't got no problem, Jules. I'm sending the Wolf." The cool comes back to Jules and he smiles. "You sending the Wolf? That's all you had to say!"

Enter Winston Wolf, or simply "the Wolf." Cool, collected, and surgically precise, the Wolf isn't there to debate the merits of the situation or make them feel better about their predicament. He's there to fix it.

Within minutes, the Wolf assesses the chaos and gets straight to work. He doesn't just issue orders—he commands respect. He knows what needs to be done, and crucially, he knows how to get others to do it. Jules and Vincent don't argue; they follow, and the mess is cleaned up and the situation is under control with minutes to spare. What makes the Wolf indispensable isn't just his expertise; it's his ability to step into the fray and do what the principals can't. He's the outside collaborator everyone dreams of when the heat is on.

In business, moments like these don't come with a cinematic soundtrack or a sleek fixer in a tuxedo. But they do come. A deal goes sideways, a critical supply chain collapses, or legal trouble threatens to derail everything. When that happens, your "Winston Wolf" might be a lawyer, a banker, a consultant, or a key vendor. These aren't just contacts you call when things go wrong—they're trusted collaborators, the kind of people who can stabilize a wobbling ship or steer you out of trouble altogether.

The best CEOs know that having these collaborators isn't enough. Relationships need tending, communication needs to be clear, and trust must be built long before you're knee-deep in chaos. The Wolf might solve problems in a pinch, but in the real world, outside collaborators are most effective when they feel like part of your team—long before you're in crisis mode. This chapter is about finding your Wolves, building relationships with them, and ensuring that when things get messy, they're ready to step in and help clean it up.

DEFINING COLLABORATORS

In the intricate web of business relationships, collaborators are your strategic partners outside the walls of your organization. They might be the attorneys who safeguard your legal standing, the bankers who keep your financial engine running, the accountants who ensure accuracy in your numbers, or the specialized consultants and vendors who bring expertise your team doesn't have in-house.

Unlike your executives or employees, collaborators aren't on your payroll, don't live within your culture, and aren't bound by your corporate hierarchy. Their priorities are shaped by their own businesses and client lists. They may be deeply committed to your success, but their loyalty isn't exclusive—they could be serving dozens of other companies at the same time.

That difference matters. Your internal team's mission is singular:

advancing your company's goals every day. Collaborators, by contrast, engage with you transactionally—even if they become trusted advisors. Their value comes from the fresh perspective, technical depth, and cross-industry experience they bring to the table. They fill critical gaps, enabling you to navigate complex challenges and seize opportunities without increasing headcount.

The best CEOs don't see collaborators as mere service providers. They treat them as partners—managing the relationship intentionally, setting clear expectations, and investing time in building trust. Done well, these relationships can amplify your reach, sharpen your decision-making, and accelerate results.

Now, let's look at the different types of collaborators you're likely to work with—and how each can play a unique role in your success.

TYPES OF COLLABORATORS

Before you can build relationships with collaborators, it's essential to assess your company's needs and identify the specific skills and resources you lack in-house. These may include legal expertise to navigate regulatory landscapes, financial acumen to manage complex transactions, or strategic vendors who offer critical products and services. Channel partners can also play a key role in extending your market reach, while accountants and bankers provide foundational support for financial stability and growth.

A CEO must take a proactive approach to determine where external expertise can make the most significant impact. Start by evaluating your company's strategic goals and pinpointing areas where internal capabilities fall short. For instance, are you entering new markets that require specialized legal advice? Do you need financial structuring for an upcoming acquisition? Understanding these gaps allows you to seek out collaborators whose expertise aligns with your objectives. This assessment is not a one-time exercise but an ongoing process that evolves with your business.

With everything, you start with the end in mind—where do you want to lead your company, what are your short- and long-term goals, and what will you need to get there? Start with where you are—what is your assessment of your current team? If you've reviewed your bosses and your team, what are your strengths and what skillsets are missing within your organization? What does your company excel at and where do you need further expertise and capacity?

What will the future of your company look like? Are you expanding into new markets or looking to implement new technology? Are you selling or buying a company? Will you need bank financing for your business?

Based on how you see the future, the types of collaborators you need will become clear.

HOW TO FIND THE BEST COLLABORATORS

Finding the right collaborators requires a deliberate and methodical approach. Begin by leveraging your professional network; referrals from trusted peers or industry contacts often lead to possible collaborators. Identify the industry veterans and "people who know" and ask them who are the best people you need to meet. Since this is a book about relationships, tap into your strongest relationships inside and outside of your company to help you.

Executives in your industry associations and trade groups can provide valuable recommendations, as can your current advisors or board members who may have insights into reputable professionals in their circles. Seek out the "name-droppers" you meet with and write down the individuals whose names you hear over and over. When talking to someone in your network, ask them, "Who else should I get to know, and can you introduce them to me?"

Once you've identified potential collaborators, set a continuous practice of always going out and meeting people and having ongoing conversations. You never know when you will need a new vendor or have to bring in a litigation attorney or some other specialist you may not have ever had a need to work with. Get to know the individuals in advance. Compatibility is key; ensure their communication style, work ethic, and approach to problem-solving align with your company's culture and needs.

It's also essential to assess their scalability and adaptability. A good collaborator will grow with your business and remain flexible as your needs evolve. If it is possible, figure out an initial engagement or project to test the waters before committing to a long-term arrangement. During this trial phase, pay close attention to their responsiveness, professionalism, and ability to deliver on promises.

There are countless outside resources that you will need to help you successfully scale your business, but below we will discuss some of the key collaborators you will certainly need to identify and work with.

STRATEGIC VENDORS

Wendel Weeks has just one framed memento on his desk, a message Steve Jobs sent him on the day the iPhone came out: "We couldn't have done it without you."

In 2007, as Steve Jobs prepared to launch the revolutionary iPhone, he faced a daunting challenge: finding a material that was durable enough to withstand daily use yet sleek enough to meet Apple's exacting design standards. Plastic wouldn't work for what Jobs envisioned. He reached out to his manufacturing partners in Asia, but they didn't have what he needed. A friend of Jobs's recommended he reach out to Corning Glass in Upstate New York, a company with a storied history of material innovation. Corning had developed Gorilla Glass years earlier but had shelved it due to lack of commercial demand.

Jobs, with his visionary foresight and relentless drive, saw its potential.

Jobs reached out directly to Wendell Weeks, Corning's CEO, with an urgent and ambitious request: produce Gorilla Glass at scale within six months. Weeks initially balked, explaining that Corning's facilities weren't equipped for such rapid production. But Jobs was undeterred.

He persuaded Weeks with his characteristic blend of charm and determination, famously declaring, "Don't be afraid. You can do this."

Under Jobs's leadership, Apple provided Corning with the financial and logistical support needed to meet the challenge. The result was nothing short of transformative. Gorilla Glass became a cornerstone of the iPhone's success, setting a new standard for smartphone durability and design. For Corning, the partnership not only revived a dormant product but also established the company as a leader in the consumer electronics space.

I love this story because it illustrates the profound impact a strategic vendor can have on a company's success. Jobs didn't just treat Corning as a supplier; he engaged them as a collaborator. By aligning their goals, fostering open communication, and providing the resources needed to achieve a shared vision, Jobs ensured that both Apple and Corning thrived. For CEOs, the lesson is clear: The right collaborator, managed effectively, can be a game changer.

I've seen too many companies leave the role of vendor engagement to the CFO or to the operations area of the business. But are the individuals you trust to manage these relationships aligned with your company's vision and actively shaping its future? They may be "beating them up" on price and have negotiated great terms, but are you truly getting the best value from these vendors and securing "favored nation" status with them? The best way to stay on top of the client list with your most important vendors is by investing in the relationship from the top of your company to the right person at your vendor.

You want to become very important to your most strategic vendors. Find out what is important to them—is it payment terms, volume, scheduling, or some other point? One thing almost all clients need is more business; let them know you can help them by offering to be a reference client. If they are important to you, offer to give a testimonial. A video of you on their website goes a long way for them. Plus, they will always have to keep the client on their homepage happy and will jump at the first take that you might not be happy anymore.

At Apollo Bank, we offered to be a "beta site" for one of our technology vendors. The vendor wanted to roll out a new product in their banking suite that they could offer to all of their banking clients. The problem was that bank technology departments don't make a purchasing and implementation decision without knowing that some other bank is using the technology first. We offered to be what they called a "Premier Partner," which gave us pricing breaks and, more importantly, access to the C-suite of their company. As their other prospects and clients came to see a demo of the product in use, we got special attention—often with the vendor's president personally on-site to show off the implementation. You can bet that all of our technology glitches and updates were resolved before their company's president stepped into our offices.

When you're willing to be an early adopter—or help a vendor shine in front of their prospects—you earn VIP treatment. You move to the top of their priority list. That's what happens when you stop acting like a customer and start acting like a partner.

THE MONEY PEOPLE

Patrick Bet-David built a national insurance firm. He knew he might want to sell it someday—but not yet. So he started meeting with investment bankers early. Just listening. Learning. Asking questions.

They told him: "Your firm's probably worth 5x EBITDA."

He thought: *Not interested.*

But instead of walking away, he leaned in. He asked what it would take to get to a higher multiple.

They told him: "Tech-enabled companies are going for 10x. But you lease your software. You don't own it."

So Bet-David built his own. He launched Bamboo, a proprietary platform for internal use and external licensing. A few years later, he sold the company—not for 5x. Not for 10x.

For 16x.

Why? Because he listened. And because he built real relationships with people who understood how value was created in his space.

That's what smart CEOs do. They don't just build companies—they build *value.*

Money doesn't grow on trees, but it is doled out by bankers—and who gets the money is determined by more art than science. Relationships are everything when you're raising capital, buying or selling a business, or trying to scale wisely.

COMMERCIAL BANKERS

As someone who founded a bank and still invests in them, here's the truth: When picking a bank, you're not choosing an institution—you're choosing a person. Your commercial banker is the one who is going to help you get the loan you need to grow your business and be your main financial partner for every part of your business such as payments and your transactional accounts. As mundane as some of these parts of your business may be, they are important enough to warrant your attention.

Pick the banker who believes in your story. A good one will know your business inside and out. They'll walk your floors, talk to your team, and root for you. They'll also know how to get things done inside their own bank. That internal influence matters more than logos or branch count.

Yes, the bank needs to have the capabilities. But it's your banker who opens doors, advocates for you in credit committees, and makes the calls when you need them.

Don't just treat them like a vendor. Give them the tour. Bring them to lunch. Let them meet your senior leadership team. Good bankers invest in relationships—they want to bet on people, not paperwork.

INVESTMENT BANKERS

If you're thinking about buying or selling—even *someday*—you need to start building relationships with investment bankers now. Investment bankers are the ones who are going to help you in a mergers and acquisitions (M&A) deal or a transaction involving raising outside capital. Don't wait until you're running a process. That's too late.

The truth is, when a deal heats up, you'll spend more time with your investment banker than with your spouse. You want to know—*deeply know*—that they're aligned with your goals, not just chasing a transaction fee.

Great investment bankers are also relationship engines. They know the buyers. The sellers. Your competitors. They see the whole chessboard.

You want them thinking of you when a deal crosses their desk. That only happens if you've invested in the relationship early. And if they believe you're serious.

ACCOUNTANTS AND TAX EXPERTS

Too many CEOs leave the relationship with outside accountants to the CFO. Don't.

If you work with a larger regional or national firm, know the partner on your account. Big firms rotate staff constantly. If you want continuity, you need to build the relationship—and make sure the partner knows you expect white-glove service.

Same goes for tax specialists. Not all accountants are tax experts. And the best tax experts are worth their weight in gold *before* a big event—like a sale, merger, or ownership transition.

Don't just talk to them once a year before filing season. Invest in the relationship. Sit down and map out your future. A great tax advisor will help you do it legally, ethically—and with maximum efficiency.

LAWYERS

A great lawyer does more than protect your downside—they can unlock your future.

You need someone who can navigate legal complexity, yes—but more importantly, someone who can make deals happen, open doors, and carry weight when it matters most.

No one embodied that better than Bill Gates Sr.

Most people know him as the father of Microsoft founder Bill Gates Jr. But in Seattle's business community, Gates Sr. was already a legend—long before his son ever wrote a line of code. He was a towering figure (literally and figuratively): an accomplished attorney, a civic leader, and the guy you called when a deal needed to get done *and* done right.

In the late 1980s, Howard Schultz had a dream. He didn't just want to sell coffee—he wanted to build a *third place* between home and work. Jazz music. Conversation. Culture. It was a vision that most Americans didn't even know they wanted yet. But Schultz could see it.

He just couldn't buy it.

At the time, Starbucks was still a small Seattle operation selling beans and brewing gear. Schultz owned a separate espresso bar concept called Il Giornale. He wanted to merge the two—to bring his vision to life—but he didn't have the money, and the Starbucks founders weren't making it easy. Worse, a wealthy local businessman had stepped in and was trying to buy the company out from under him.

So Schultz picked up the phone and called Gates Sr.

Gates didn't just offer legal advice—he stepped into the middle of the deal and brought with him a level of credibility, influence, and calm that changed everything. He met with the Starbucks founders. He reassured Schultz's investors. He even had what Schultz later described as a *"quiet but pointed"* conversation with the rival bidder. Soon after, that rival quietly exited the picture.

With Gates Sr. in the room, everything changed. He wasn't loud. He wasn't flashy. But people listened. And they trusted him.

The deal got done. Schultz bought Starbucks for $3.8 million, and the rest is history. But none of it happened without a lawyer who did more than draft contracts. Gates Sr. played the role every CEO dreams of in a legal partner: trusted advisor, calm in the storm, and a deal closer with real presence.

That's the kind of lawyer you want by your side.

Not all lawyers are created equal. You need the right legal bench. At minimum, that includes:

- A go-to general corporate advisor
- A specialist in litigation, if needed
- Experts for industry-specific or high-stakes transactions

Don't assume your lawyer has all the answers. And don't assume the "best" lawyer is the one with the highest hourly rate or biggest firm name.

Watch how they work. Do they return your call—or delegate you to an associate? Do they know your business—or just read your documents? Do they treat your team with respect—or just save that tone for you?

Also: Lawyers who treat everything like a courtroom fight may not be the best fit for business. Sometimes you need a scalpel, not a sword. Sometimes you need someone who can read the room, not just the statute.

Legal issues are inevitable. Litigation might come. Deals will happen. When they do, you want a lawyer who doesn't just protect the downside—but helps you seize the upside. Find your Gates Sr.

A good lawyer protects your blind side. But to grow, you need partners who expand your reach. In most businesses, that means distributors—the people who carry your product, advocate for it, and get it in front of customers you could never reach alone. These relationships aren't about contracts; they're about alignment, trust, and shared momentum.

DISTRIBUTORS AND CHANNEL PARTNERS

In many businesses, the company producing a product doesn't sell directly to its end customer—they have to work through distributors or channel partners. These partners are the ones with the shelf space, the buyer relationships, or the customer access your company can't easily replicate. In some industries, these relationships are the lifeblood of the business.

When it works, it can be transformational. Just ask Spindrift.

Spindrift, a small sparkling water company founded in 2010, set out to disrupt the beverage market with its distinctive approach: sparkling water made with real fruit juice. Competing against titans like LaCroix and Coca-Cola required ingenuity—not just in product design but in distribution strategy.

Early on, Spindrift struggled to secure shelf space in national grocery chains. They turned to UNFI (United Natural Foods, Inc.), a leading distributor specializing in natural and organic products. UNFI gave them access to health-conscious consumers through a trusted network of retailers. It wasn't just about logistics—it was about shared values and aligned missions. CEO Bill Creelman worked closely with UNFI to craft a plan that fit Spindrift's identity, and the result was explosive growth and national recognition.

But not every brand nails this.

Honest Tea, co-founded by Seth Goldman, built its reputation as an organic, low-sugar alternative to mainstream bottled drinks. It had loyal customers and a strong brand identity—but it ran into trouble with its distribution.

After Coca-Cola acquired Honest Tea in stages beginning in 2008, the brand gained access to the beverage giant's powerful distribution network. On paper, this was a dream scenario: massive reach, better shelf placement, and serious scale. But the cultural fit wasn't there. Honest Tea relied on storytelling, local appeal, and shelf-level education—none of which translated well in Coke's high-volume, low-touch sales model.

Distributors began to deprioritize Honest Tea in favor of better-known, faster-moving products. Communication broke down. Honest Tea didn't get the attention it once had with independent distributors, and Coca-Cola's team didn't have the bandwidth—or incentive—to champion a niche brand. In 2022, Coca-Cola discontinued Honest Tea altogether, citing supply chain constraints and prioritization of other brands. What had once been a rising star was quietly shelved.

Bigger isn't always better. If your distributor doesn't understand your brand or share your priorities, your product becomes just another

SKU—and that's when things fall apart. You need channel partners who see your success as their success, not just more boxes on a truck.

The same truth applies beyond distribution. Every external partner—whether they move your product, represent your brand, or advise your strategy—carries real relational weight. The wrong partner can slow you down; the right one can change your trajectory. Consultants fall squarely into this category. They bring expertise your team may lack, but only if you manage the relationship with the same clarity and discipline you bring to any strategic alliance.

CONSULTANTS

In building a business, you'll inevitably reach a point where your internal team can't do it all. You'll need more management bandwidth or deeper expertise in areas like operations, IT, HR, or finance—skills that your people don't yet have or simply don't have time to develop. That's when consultants come in. One quarter, it might be an operations specialist helping you redesign workflow, the next, a marketing strategist building your brand story, or an HR expert tightening your compensation plan and hiring process.

Hiring and managing consultants can be overwhelming. You'll interact with many, but only a few are worth developing real relationships with. The key is deciding where to invest that time. I've learned that the best consultants—regardless of specialty—have one thing in common: They tell you the truth, even when it's uncomfortable. Set that tone early. Tell them you'll always value candor over flattery, and then prove it by honoring them when they do it.

One of the biggest risks in bringing in consultants is the threat of "scope creep." Most consultants are going to charge you on an hourly basis and the only way you can make more money is by doing more work and staying at your firm longer. Beware the "burrower"—the consultants who dig into your company so deep you can never get rid of them. The ones where the project is never complete and they've turned a short-term assignment into a full-time job.

When working with consultants who are in your business, the delicate balance is in not letting your team think you are undermining them or that you trust an outsider more than you trust your team. You do this by making sure the consultants truly are specialists and experts—top in their field with an expertise everyone agrees you don't have internally.

BUILDING AND KEEPING STRONG RELATIONSHIPS WITH COLLABORATORS

Once you've found great collaborators, the work isn't over—it's just beginning. Relationships, even with outside partners, need maintenance. You can't just call in your lawyer when things go sideways, or expect your banker to move mountains if you've been MIA for two years. The best CEOs I know build long-term, high-trust relationships with their collaborators—and treat them like extensions of their internal team. That doesn't mean micromanaging them. It means being intentional, communicative, and consistent. Here's how you do it.

1. **Define expectations clearly.** At the outset of any relationship, be explicit about your goals, timelines, and expectations. A clear scope of work prevents misunderstandings and ensures alignment.
2. **Communicate regularly.** Don't let the absence of formal reporting structures lead to sporadic communication. Schedule regular check-ins to stay updated, provide feedback, and keep the relationship on track.
3. **Respect their expertise.** Collaborators are specialists for a reason. Trust their recommendations and give them the autonomy to deliver their best work. Micromanaging them undermines their value.
4. **Invest in relationships, not just transactions.** Take the time to know your collaborators personally. Build rapport beyond the work at hand. A strong personal connection can lead to greater commitment and willingness to go the extra mile.

5. **Pay promptly and fairly.** A surefire way to sour a relationship is to delay payments or haggle excessively. Demonstrating respect for their time and effort through prompt and fair payment builds goodwill.
6. **Be a partner, not just a client.** Provide value in return. Share referrals, offer testimonials, and advocate for their services when appropriate. Reciprocity strengthens the bond.
7. **Evaluate and provide feedback.** Periodically assess the relationship's effectiveness. Constructive feedback helps collaborators refine their approach to meet your needs better.
8. **Adapt to changing needs.** Your business evolves, and so will your requirements from collaborators. Keep them informed about changes in your strategy or operations so they can adapt their support accordingly.
9. **Maintain transparency.** Be up-front about challenges or concerns. A collaborative relationship thrives on openness and honesty.
10. **End relationships gracefully.** Not all collaborations will last forever, and that's okay. If you need to move on, handle it professionally. Leave the door open for future opportunities.

As CEO, you're the steward of all relationships critical to your company's success, including those with collaborators. Your ability to engage and inspire external partners sets the tone for the entire organization. When you treat collaborators as integral members of your extended team, you foster a culture of respect and excellence that radiates outward.

In the end, the strength of your collaborator relationships isn't just about achieving operational efficiency or meeting immediate needs. It's about creating a network of trusted allies who amplify your capabilities and enable you to scale heights that no single organization can reach alone.

In the next chapter we will look beyond the operations of your business to the broader world of where you live, where you compete, and people that you interact with—we will call this *the community.*

Before you move on, take five minutes to assess your key outside collaborators:

- Who are the three to five most important external partners I rely on today?
- Do they know how important they are to me?
- When's the last time I talked to them—outside a transaction or issue?
- If I had a crisis tomorrow, who would I call first?

If you're not confident in the answers, you've got relationship work to do.

KEY TAKEAWAYS

- **Find your wolves.** Know exactly who you will call before things go sideways, because in moments of pressure, preparation beats improvisation.
- **Partners, not vendors.** The right collaborators don't just execute tasks; they strengthen your judgment, sharpen your decisions, and expand what's possible.
- **Listen to the people who know.** When you truly trust your bankers, lawyers, and accountants, you stop using them as transaction processors and start using them as strategic advisors.
- **It's not just what they do—it's what they unlock.** Great collaborators give you access to relationships, credibility, and opportunities you could never create on your own.

Chapter 4

THE COMMUNITY

Mike Ovitz understood something most of his competitors didn't: Relationships weren't just part of the business—they *were* the business.

In Hollywood, everyone wanted to be your best friend until the next big deal came through. Ovitz refused to play that game. He wasn't chasing transactional handshakes or empty charm. His approach was quieter, deeper, and far more strategic.

For Ovitz, building an empire like Creative Artists Agency (CAA) meant building an ecosystem—one that reached far beyond studio lots and red carpets. He embedded himself in the very institutions that shaped Los Angeles: the schools, the museums, the hospitals, even city hall. He didn't just represent stars; he became part of the architecture of their lives.

While other agents were handing out Lakers tickets or calling in favors for a reservation at Spago, Ovitz was thinking long term. He made sure his clients' kids got into Harvard-Westlake. He turned museum donations into acts of civic sainthood. He positioned his clients' names beside Spielberg's on the Cedars-Sinai donor wall.

This was more than representation—it was life curation.

The brilliance of it was subtle. Ovitz never had to remind anyone of his value. His influence was visible everywhere. Each introduction, each philanthropic gesture, each discreet favor was another thread binding him to the people who mattered most to his business.

To him, this wasn't about performative altruism; it was about connection. Every hospital wing he helped fund, every art exhibit he championed, every board he quietly joined didn't just serve Los Angeles—it deepened the bond between him and his clients. He wasn't merely their agent; he was their confidant, their fixer, their first call when life got complicated.

So when a rival agent came sniffing around with promises of bigger deals, it rarely mattered. Ovitz's clients weren't loyal because of contracts. They were loyal because he had woven himself into the fabric of their lives.

That was his genius. Ovitz didn't treat relationships as tools to repair something when it broke; he built them as the foundation of everything he created. In a world as ruthless as Hollywood, he understood that the real power wasn't in the deal—it was in the depth of connection. The deeper those ties ran, the harder it was for anyone else to touch you.

While competitors sipped martinis and chased headlines, Ovitz invested in Los Angeles itself—the schools where his clients' children studied, the galleries that doubled as networking salons, the hospitals where gratitude came with naming rights. He knew that if you could root yourself in the institutions of a city, you weren't just an agent anymore. You were a civic pillar.

When you become indispensable to the community, you become indispensable to everyone who depends on it.

In this chapter, we'll explore how to cultivate this kind of community-based power. Building these relationships doesn't only shield your company during hard times; it fortifies your presence in a way that competitors can't easily replicate. By embedding yourself within the broader community, you gain allies in places most CEOs rarely consider.

THE PERSONAL POWER NETWORK

Just as Mike Ovitz embedded himself into the core institutions of Los Angeles, you too can cultivate your own web of professional allies. These aren't just business cards or LinkedIn connections—they're part of your industry's human infrastructure. Competitors, friendly rivals, and industry groups all play a role in shaping your company's environment. While they might wear different jerseys, they're all playing the same game. The trick is learning how to work with, learn from, and even lean on these players without compromising your edge.

COMPETITORS

The idea of sitting down for coffee with your competitor might sound like sharing a foxhole with the enemy. But in a world of shared challenges and mutual interests, it's a strategic imperative.

Market-shaping events, new regulations, reputational threats—these things don't just hit you. They hit everyone in your space. When that happens, your fiercest rival might be your best ally.

In Michael Mann's film *Heat*, Al Pacino plays a hardened cop. Robert De Niro plays a professional thief. They sit across from each other in a diner—cop and criminal—and talk. They respect each other. They size each other up. They know what they're both capable of. And more than anything, they want to understand what the other is thinking. That's what this kind of relationship is like. You don't have to be friends. But if you understand each other, you're both better off.

You don't share your playbook. But you share just enough to make the whole system better:

- You learn who to avoid in the vendor world.
- You swap insights on labor shortages or regulation.
- You stay ahead of market forces that affect you both.

Jim Collins talks about "productive paranoia"—being aware of what's around the corner. Competitor conversations can give you that edge. They won't give you their secrets, and you won't give yours. But you'll both see around the bend a little better.

And when a crisis hits your industry, your competitor might be the only one who truly understands what you're up against.

Some competitors are more than rivals—they're worthy of admiration. Simon Sinek calls them "worthy rivals"—those who challenge us to raise our game.

Bill Belichick and Nick Saban are two of the most successful football coaches of all time. One in the NFL, one in college. But they spent every offseason together—sharing ideas, breaking down tape, swapping stories. Not because they weren't competitive, but because they respected the game—and each other—enough to keep learning.

I had a similar experience starting Apollo Bank. I didn't know how to start a bank—so I called forty people who did. One call led to another. I wasn't trying to steal resources. I was trying to understand the path. People shared generously. Why? Because I showed up with humility and curiosity.

One of my fiercest local competitors, David Seleski, turned out to be one of my best teachers. He ran a bigger, more established bank. I asked to visit. He welcomed me. He walked me through his systems, his lessons, his approach. He didn't lose anything by helping me. But I gained a lot. That's the kind of relationship that makes your entire sector better.

Clay Christensen, the late Harvard Business School professor and author of *The Innovator's Dilemma*, revolutionized how we think about disruption in business. He taught that breakthrough innovation often comes from the edges—from new players who see things differently. Christensen reminds us that real learning often comes from unexpected sources—including your competitors. A worthy rival might be the very person who's already figured out what you're struggling with. But if your pride gets in the way, you'll miss the opportunity to grow.

If you want to build relationships with worthy rivals:

- **Look outside your city or state.** A little geographic distance makes it easier to share ideas freely without the fear of direct competition.
- **Find someone doing what you're trying to do, but better.** Seek out those who challenge and inspire you—they're often the best teachers.
- **Ask questions. Share your story. Be open.** Vulnerability invites generosity. Show you're not there to compete, but to learn.
- **Always ask: "Who else should I meet?"** The best introductions come through trusted networks. Each connection leads to another—and the next one might be gold.

These aren't just tips for networking. They're habits of humility and curiosity. And they'll make you better.

INDUSTRY ASSOCIATIONS

Industry associations rarely make headlines. But they shape the ones you eventually appear in.

Marshall Goldsmith, a world-renowned executive coach and author of *What Got You Here Won't Get You There*, reminds us that past success doesn't guarantee future relevance. That message should ring loud for any CEO navigating a fast-changing landscape. Industry associations offer a vital window into what's next—emerging trends, policy shifts, innovations—that could disrupt or accelerate your business.

Goldsmith's advice is simple but profound: What made you successful yesterday could be the very thing holding you back tomorrow. Industry associations help keep you ahead of that curve by expanding your vision, connecting you to peers, and pulling you out of your company echo chamber. They're not just slow-moving bureaucracies—they're long-range radar systems for your industry.

Don't just pay your association dues. Lead. Show up. Speak at events. Sit on a committee. Encourage your team to get involved. When you're visible in your industry, your credibility multiplies.

And don't just show up when there's a crisis. The time to build these relationships is before you need them. That way, when the crisis comes, you're not just another voice in the crowd—you're already on the board.

Here's a practical tactic: Treat every industry conference like an opportunity to host your own curated dinner. Reach out to five to seven people before the event, pick a great restaurant, and make it memorable. Relationships aren't built over free cocktails. They're built over real conversations in great company.

Trade associations are your best source for:

- Advocacy on regulation
- Peer learning
- Access to vendor and partner recommendations
- Emerging trend insight

They're slow-moving, yes—but they're powerful. If you help steer the ship, it'll move in your direction.

We've covered the insiders—your competitors, peers, and trade groups. Now we're stepping outside your industry and into the civic and institutional world that shapes the terrain your business runs on.

THE INSTITUTIONAL POWER NETWORK

In the high-stakes world of stadium politics, few stories show the power of proximity better than the saga between Washington, DC, and Ted Leonsis—the billionaire owner of the Washington Wizards and Capitals.

For years, Leonsis envisioned a new, state-of-the-art arena to anchor downtown DC—not just as a sports venue, but as a catalyst for jobs, tourism, and community pride. He wanted the teams to stay rooted in the city.

When talks with Mayor Muriel Bowser's administration stalled over funding and structure, Virginia swooped in with promises: a modern arena, infrastructure upgrades, and lucrative incentives. On paper, it looked unbeatable. In reality, something was missing—connection. Meetings were delayed, details stayed vague, and Richmond's dealmakers never built real rapport with Leonsis. As he later admitted, "There were moments I felt like we weren't being taken seriously."

Bowser took the opposite approach. Even in deadlock, she kept showing up—calling, meeting, listening. They didn't always agree, but she understood deals aren't just done in conference rooms. They're forged inside conversations, quiet reassurances, and years of accumulated trust.

When Virginia's proposal collapsed, DC was ready. With renewed trust and clearer terms, the two sides reached a deal worth hundreds of millions in public-private investment—keeping the teams downtown and securing a long-term economic engine for the city.

Your institutional power network is about the people and institutions shaping the environment your business operates in—government officials, universities, nonprofits. They may not sign your checks, but they can move the goalposts. And if you build relationships early, they'll move them in your favor.

They're the city commissioners deciding where your business can expand. They're the university administrators shaping the talent pipeline. They're the nonprofit leaders rallying public opinion around the causes that define your brand's reputation—whether you're involved or not.

These relationships might feel one step removed from your day-to-day operations, but in many ways, they're the scaffolding that holds your company up. And when things shift—when zoning laws change, when public opinion turns, when the talent pool dries up—having the right institutional relationships can make the difference between reacting too late or shaping the outcome from the start.

Let's explore how to build smart, lasting relationships with three core types of institutions: government, academia, and nonprofit organizations.

GOVERNMENT

Every business operates within a framework of rules, incentives, and infrastructure—and the government shapes all three. Yet, many CEOs treat government relationships as a burden to manage, rather than an opportunity to lead.

The truth is, every policy, regulation, and public investment decision affects your company's future. Whether it's zoning for your next expansion, tax credits for innovation, or partnerships on community development, the government can be a powerful ally—or an invisible obstacle—depending on the relationships you build.

The best CEOs don't just show up when they need something. They cultivate genuine, long-term relationships with public officials, agency leaders, and policymakers who influence their industry. They learn the language of public interest, align their goals with civic priorities, and look for opportunities where business success and community good intersect.

What building government relationships looks like in practice:

- Attend civic events, council meetings, or public hearings—especially when they don't directly involve you.
- Proactively meet with local and state officials to understand their priorities.
- Offer support for community initiatives that align with your values.
- Keep communication open during both good and challenging times.
- Be a constructive, consistent presence—so when an opportunity or crisis arises, you're already at the table.

Working with the government isn't just about politics—it's about proximity. Show up early, stay engaged, and earn trust long before you need something.

ACADEMIA

Every business needs talent. Every business needs ideas. And most CEOs look too far and too wide when both might be right down the street at the local university.

Academic institutions are often overlooked by CEOs—not because they lack value, but because they don't look or act like a normal business. But they're shaping the workforce, conducting research, and experimenting with the technologies and business models that could either disrupt your company or unlock your next chapter.

Academic institutions are more than just research hubs and talent pools—they're untapped engines of innovation and influence. But only if you build the relationship.

The smart move for a CEO is to go beyond just recruiting on campus; you want to get plugged into the ecosystem:

- **Connect with the career center:** Use it to build a steady internship or talent pipeline.
- **Partner with specific departments:** Choose a field of study—engineering, finance, marketing—that matches your business.
- **Sponsor student projects or research:** Offer guest lectures. Open your doors for plant or office tours.
- **Invest in small-scale support:** Choose a student competition, a niche program, or a speaker series—that aligns with your values.

You don't need a seven-figure check to make a difference. Sometimes, just showing up regularly with time, attention, and curiosity is enough to build lasting credibility. And yes, when the time is right—make the donation. It doesn't just support education. It roots your company in the community and signals that you're not just here for profits—you're here to serve as a cornerstone of the community.

NONPROFITS

If academia is the pipeline of ideas, nonprofits are the conscience of your community. They do what your company can't do alone—support the underserved, enrich the community's soul, address systemic challenges. When you engage sincerely with the right nonprofits, they become more than feel-good allies—they become strategic partners.

Getting involved with nonprofits helps your company:

- Attract talent who care about more than a paycheck.
- Build goodwill in the community.
- Give your leaders a training ground outside of day-to-day business.

Board service is one of the best leadership labs out there. You learn diplomacy, fundraising, volunteer management, public speaking, and navigating difficult dynamics. And you meet other civic-minded business leaders who see your values in action.

Here's how to do it well:

- Pick causes aligned with your values—and those of your team.
- Show up personally. Don't just write checks.
- Encourage team members to serve on boards or volunteer. Recognize and support their efforts.
- Partner with nonprofits to create win–win community impact—joint events, shared services, awareness campaigns.

Jim Collins wrote about "Level 5 leadership"—a blend of humility and fierce resolve. Supporting nonprofits gives your company a chance to live out those traits. Not performatively. But powerfully. And when people see you giving, listening, and working alongside others—not for profit, but for purpose—they'll remember.

THE PUBLIC POWER NETWORK

A few years ago, a client of mine, a midsize construction firm won the bid to renovate a historic downtown building. This wasn't just another job—this was *the* building. Old brick, city landmark, generations of family photos taken in front of it. The mayor cared. The preservation groups cared. The neighborhood Facebook groups definitely cared.

Halfway through demolition, a photo started circulating online: a pile of what looked like ornate stonework tossed into a dumpster. Within hours, the story hardened into outrage. "Local developer destroys historic facade for profit." People who had never heard of the company suddenly had an opinion about its ethics.

Here's the problem: The photo wasn't what it looked like. The stone wasn't original—it was a cheap 1970s add-on that the city had already approved for removal. The company had actually been the one pushing to restore the *true* original facade.

But because the company hadn't built any real relationship with the local paper, the preservation nonprofit, or the neighborhood association, there was no one to slow the fire down. The first version of the story became *the* story. The CEO ended up spending weeks doing cleanup with city council, the historical board, and angry residents—all to prove they weren't the villains they'd been painted to be in twelve hours.

Perception isn't everything, but it's not far behind. You can have the best product, the strongest numbers, and the happiest customers, but if your community doesn't know about it, believe it, or feel it, it won't matter. Reputation compounds. That's why every CEO needs to think seriously about their public power network—the media, the trade publications, and the influencers who help shape the narrative around your business.

MEDIA

Local journalists, industry reporters, and even bloggers have the power to make, or complicate, your story. They're not your marketing team, but they're a critical part of your ecosystem. When you treat them like partners—not pests—you can build a relationship that pays off.

Here's the biggest mistake I see CEOs make when working on their media outreach: They call the media only when they want coverage. That doesn't work. Build the relationship before you need it.

- Be a resource, not a pitch machine. Share trends. Offer commentary. Send them useful data even when it's not about you.
- Know their deadlines. Know their beat. Know their name.
- Return calls. Answer emails. Be someone they trust.

One underrated tactic that has worked for me over the years is to notice effort, even when it has nothing to do with your company. Praise their work. If a reporter covers something insightful, send a quick note. Post it. Tag them. Most people only reach out when they want something. Be the person who reaches out just to say "nice job."

The best CEOs build relationships with local business reporters and trade editors by being accessible, smart, and generous with insights. When the time comes to tell their own story—a new product, a milestone, a shift in strategy—those relationships make all the difference in getting the word out in the most positive light.

TRADE PUBLICATIONS

While mainstream media shapes broad perception, trade publications shape insider reputation. If you want to be known in your sector, start here.

Pitch op-eds. Speak at industry webinars. Comment on trends. Become a name that shows up in their coverage—not because you asked, but because you earned it.

Your future collaborators, investors, and employees read these publications to figure out who matters. If you're invisible here, you're invisible to the people who matter most.

Finding the right publications:

- Look for the outlets your peers, competitors, and industry leaders actually read and reference. Ask these people what they subscribe to and read; notice which publications they are following on LinkedIn.
- Check which publications sponsor major industry events or partner with respected trade associations.
- See where influential people in your space are quoted, profiled, or contributing.
- Prioritize publications with strong editorial standards and broad reach in your sector—not just vanity blogs or pay-to-play outlets.

Earning meaningful coverage:

- Build relationships with editors and journalists before you pitch. Comment on their articles, share their work, and offer insights they can use.
- Provide unique data, case studies, or perspectives that add value to their audience.
- Offer yourself as an expert source when trends, challenges, or breaking news stories hit your industry.
- Be consistent—submit articles, insights, and commentary over time so your name becomes familiar.
- Focus on educating, not selling; credibility comes from being useful, not self-promotional.

If you want to be known in your industry, you can't treat trade publications as a one-off PR play. Show up regularly, add value to the conversation, and over time, you won't have to chase coverage—it will come to you.

SOCIAL MEDIA AND INFLUENCERS

You don't need to go viral. You just need to be intentional.

Social media has flattened the hierarchy. A single Instagram story or LinkedIn post can reshape perception—for better or worse. Don't delegate this entirely to marketing. As CEO, your presence online—even if limited—sends a signal.

- Be thoughtful. Don't post for the sake of it.
- Highlight your team, your partners, your values.
- Share real stories, not corporate speak.

Influencers are a newer piece of this puzzle, and they matter more every day because they've become trusted curators in a noisy digital world. People increasingly filter their decisions through the voices they follow—whether that's choosing a restaurant, a software platform, or a financial advisor. The right influencer already has the trust and attention of the audience you want to reach, and that credibility transfers when they talk about you.

Identify the credible voices in your niche. Don't just pitch them—build a relationship. Engage. Comment. Offer value. Let them know you exist. By building the right relationships, when the time comes to amplify a product or respond to an issue, they'll already know you're someone worth listening to.

Your community isn't just your zip code—it's your industry peers, local institutions, civic leaders, media voices, and everyday neighbors. It's the air your company breathes. You don't need to dominate the landscape, but you do need to be known, trusted, and—ideally—missed if you were gone. Show up. Follow through. Be helpful.

Mike Ovitz didn't become a power broker in Los Angeles by chasing headlines. He embedded himself in the city's institutions, shaping the terrain beneath his business. That's your job, too—to build an ecosystem where your company can flourish. When you're trusted by rivals, respected by institutions, and visible in the public eye, you're not just surviving—you're influencing the game itself.

Next, we'll turn to the relationship that tests all of this work: *your customers.*

QUICK RELATIONSHIP AUDIT

Ask yourself:

- Who are the three competitors I could learn from right now?
- Which trade group or association should I get more involved in?
- Do I know my local government rep—and do they know me?
- Which nonprofit aligns with our values—and how could I get involved?
- When's the last time I spoke with a journalist, publisher, or industry influencer?

KEY TAKEAWAYS

- **Community relationships are a strategic asset.** Do not view community outreach as a feel-good extra, but as a critical way to build relationships that matter.
- **Your competitors aren't always enemies.** Find your worthy rivals and learn from them.
- **Local institutions shape the rules of the game.** Know the people, learn the rules.
- **Visibility builds trust.** Participation builds power.
- **Reputation isn't controlled—it's cultivated.** Your community should understand what you stand for and where you are willing to invest.

Chapter 5

THE CUSTOMER

In the summer of 2014, thousands of Metallica fans packed into a Stockholm arena, buzzing with anticipation—not just for the music, but for something extraordinary. This wasn't going to be an ordinary concert. For the first time, fans had voted on the setlist. Lars Ulrich, the band's legendary drummer, walked onstage and grinned. "You guys picked these songs," he said, gesturing to the crowd. "So if it sucks tonight, it's your fault." The arena roared with laughter, and then, with the opening riff of "Master of Puppets," the show was on!

This was the *Metallica by Request* tour, a bold experiment in giving their fans unprecedented control over their experience. For Metallica, it wasn't just a tour; it was a statement: *We see you. You matter.* And for the fans—some of whom had followed the band across continents—it was proof that their loyalty was more than a transaction. "I've been to fifty shows," said a fan from Germany, waving his handmade Metallica flag. "This band makes you feel like family."

Metallica's ability to foster this kind of devotion isn't an accident. It's the result of a deliberate strategy to differentiate the customer experience, treating their most loyal fans not as mere consumers but as essential members of a community. They've spent millions of dollars—and just as many hours—building these connections, from exclusive events for members of their *Fifth Member* fan club to surprise pop-up gigs in intimate venues.

For CEOs, Metallica's story is more than a rock and roll fairy tale. It's a blueprint for creating unshakable loyalty in a crowded marketplace. At the heart of their strategy lies a simple but profound principle: If you want customers to stand by you for decades, you have to make them feel seen, heard, and valued. As James Hetfield, the band's lead singer, once said, "Our fans are the reason we're still here. They're not just listening to our music—they're part of it."

Metallica didn't just sell records—they built a relationship. One forged through authenticity, access, and attention to detail. They understand something every CEO needs to grasp: In a world where loyalty is fleeting and customers have infinite choices, the product isn't enough. The companies that win are the ones that create real, lasting connections with their customers. And those connections start at the top. In this chapter, we'll look at how CEOs can build customer loyalty—not by being everywhere, but by showing up in the right moments, in the right way. We'll cover when to step in personally, how to use your time strategically, how to spot the customers who matter most, and how to create systems that embed customer obsession into your company's culture. This isn't about customer service—it's about leadership.

SETTING THE EXAMPLE FOR THE ORGANIZATION

There was a TV commercial that left a profound impact on me early in my career, shaping how I think about leadership and the role of a CEO in critical moments. While many of you may be too young to remember it—and likely don't have access to YouTube right now—I want to share its story here because the lesson it conveys about showing up for your clients is just as relevant today as it was back then.

Picture a dimly lit conference room in the late 1980s, perched on the top floor of a sprawling industrial facility. The walls are bare, functional, with large windows that hint at the hum of manufacturing below. The air is thick with tension. At the head of the table stands Ben, the company's CEO. His voice is calm but unrelenting as he addresses his team, delivering the kind of news no executive wants to hear: "I got a call this morning from one of our oldest customers. He fired us. After twenty years, he fired us." He pauses, letting the weight of those words settle.

The room is silent, save for the faint hum of the air-conditioning. Ben recounts the conversation. The client's words were a dagger: "He said he doesn't know us anymore." It wasn't about price or product; it was about being ignored, undervalued, invisible. Ben scans the faces of his management team, eyes filled with disbelief and unease. For a moment, it seems as though no one will dare speak.

Then Ben moves, striding purposefully to his assistant who hands him a stack of airline tickets. "Well folks, some things have to change; that's why we gotta get out with a little face-to-face and talk to every customer we have," he says, handing each employee in the room a ticket, tickets he points out, to visit clients in over two hundred cities. The solution isn't a memo or a quarterly meeting. It's something more visceral, something more human. As he's passing out the tickets you can see in his energy what he is telling his team: *Go see your clients. Shake their hands. Look them in the eye. Remind them they matter.*

One manager, uneasy but curious, finally breaks the silence. "Ben, where are you going?" The question lingers, and for a beat, it seems as though the CEO might brush it off, let his managers carry the burden. But Ben doesn't delegate. He doesn't deflect. His answer is as decisive as it is revealing: "To visit that old friend that fired us this morning."

And just like that, the room shifts. As Gershwin's *Rhapsody in Blue* crescendos in the background, the message is driven home with Gene Hackman's gravelly narration: "United Airlines—because the world still works better when we're face-to-face."

This isn't a story about a team being told to fix things; it's about a leader stepping into the storm. Ben's declaration signals what great leaders understand instinctively: *Some moments are too critical to outsource.* Whether it's a dissatisfied customer or a fraying relationship, these are the moments that demand the CEO's personal touch—the courage to face discomfort, own mistakes, and rebuild trust.

A CEO's time is scarce, but where you choose to show up sends a message to your entire organization. If you want your company to value customer relationships, you have to model that behavior yourself. That might mean visiting top accounts in person, personally calling a dissatisfied client, or surprising a long-time customer with a genuine thank-you gift. These moments aren't just acts of good-will—they're a blueprint for how you expect your people to listen, respond, and lead.

The most customer-centric cultures don't start in the sales department—they start with the CEO. Your actions set the tone. Your presence shows what matters. And your willingness to step out from behind the desk reminds everyone—inside and outside the company—that relationships aren't a department. They're the business itself.

The way a CEO shows up for customers becomes the cultural blueprint for the entire company—embedding relational leadership into how every employee thinks, speaks, and acts.

YOU SET THE CULTURE

Culture is a funny thing. You can't see it, touch it, or measure it on a balance sheet, but it runs through every corner of a company like electricity. And no one wires the system quite like the CEO. It's in the words they choose when speaking to and about a customer or sitting quietly in a listening session with frontline employees. Moments like those are culture-defining signals. When the CEO shows that customer relationships are worth their limited time and undivided attention, it sets a tone that resonates throughout the organization. Employees start to mirror what they see: If the leader cares deeply about customers, so will the team.

The leader needs to always model curiosity and empathy. A CEO who approaches customer interactions with a learning mindset—asking thoughtful questions, genuinely engaging with challenges, and listening more than they speak—creates a ripple effect. Customers feel heard, employees notice, and the company as a whole begins to internalize the message that every customer's time is as valuable as the CEO's.

It's not enough for the CEO to quietly embody these values, they have to broadcast them. When a CEO returns from a customer meeting and shares the experience in a team meeting, saying, "I heard this straight from the horse's mouth," it's like flipping on a spotlight. It puts the customer at the center of the conversation and reinforces a customer-centric culture in a way no memo ever could.

Transparency and accountability are vital pieces to the puzzle. A CEO who openly acknowledges where the company can improve, based on real customer feedback, sets a standard for honesty and continuous improvement. That kind of openness builds trust—not just with customers but within the organization itself.

Ultimately, no single CEO can build every customer relationship. But by modeling the behavior they want to see and empowering senior leaders to do the same, the CEO ensures that a customer-first culture permeates the business. The tone they set becomes the standard, and the culture they cultivate becomes the company's greatest asset. But where should the CEO spend their time?

A CEO'S TIME IS THE ORGANIZATION'S MOST VALUABLE RESOURCE

For a CEO, time is the most finite—and most valuable—resource. If you are reckless with your time, you'll find yourself mired in meetings that should've been emails or tangled in crises someone else could've solved. When time is spent wisely, those rare hours you dedicate to customer engagement can create a gravitational pull that aligns the entire organization around what truly matters. It's not about being everywhere, shaking every hand; it's about being in the right place, at the right time, with the right people. The question for CEOs isn't if they should engage with customers—it's how and where they can make the most impact.

In my years of experience and working with and observing top-performing leaders, here are insights about the highest-payoff activities for CEOs in building customer relationships:

STRATEGIC CUSTOMER ENGAGEMENTS

The most obvious time and place for you to get involved is on "game day"—the big opportunity pitches, when it is time to close a deal, or to sit down with the decision-makers at your biggest and best client offices. These types of interactions and opportunities are not to be left for the second tier at your organization if they are interactions and relationships that have the biggest impact on your company. You need to prioritize interactions with high-value customers (e.g., major revenue contributors, strategic partnerships). Although meeting with these types of clients at the right time is important, you need to make sure these high-value relationships are regularly nurtured—schedule time for quarterly calls or meetings with top-tier customers to gain insights and build trust.

FIELD SALES CALLS

Jamie Dimon, CEO of JPMorgan Chase, says the favorite part of his job is when he goes on field sales calls with his team. He gets to meet with customers, face-to-face, and learn about what's happening in the market and how his company is doing. Every year, in his annual shareholder letter, Dimon emphasizes the importance of visiting with his customers at their place of business and how he will never stop doing this as long as he is CEO.

Visiting customers matters. But it's not just because it strengthens the relationships with your customers and helps inform you about customer service and market conditions; it's because it gives you a great way to develop and coach your team.

Great CEOs dedicate time to shadow frontline employees like sales reps or customer service agents to better understand customer pain points and opportunities. Being alongside your sales team in the field is a great way to coach and train your employees and sets the tone across the organization. But don't underestimate what happens in the car ride home. That's where real coaching happens—when the meeting is over, the windows are down, and the feedback is honest.

CRITICAL CUSTOMER MOMENTS

Every customer relationship has its "make-or-break" moment—the point where they decide if they'll stick with you or walk away. That's where CEOs earn their keep. These are the pivotal interactions that define a customer's perception of your company—whether it's a crisis that demands immediate attention or an opportunity to exceed expectations. As in the example of Ben in the United Airlines commercial, you want to get involved when things are not going very well. A CEO should intervene personally in high-stakes situations, such as retaining a dissatisfied but influential client. You want to show the people in your company and your clients that when the going gets tough, you show up.

But bad times aren't the only times you should show up—surprise and delight customers with unexpected outreach, such as acknowledging a major milestone or resolving a long-standing issue.

CUSTOMER ADVISORY BOARDS AND CUSTOMER ENGAGEMENT EVENTS

A great way to maximize your time is by convening larger groups of customers where you can provide a great experience and engage with them firsthand. Some companies establish customer advisory boards, where a hand-selected group of key clients are gathered one or more times a year to participate in forums where customers can provide direct feedback to the CEO and leadership team. Hosting your own customer events such as user conferences, product rollouts, or other types of events where lots of customers gather in one place is a great place for the CEO to be seen and engage with customers.

The temptation is always there: to step in, to fix, to micromanage every customer complaint that bubbles up to the top. But this is a trap—a rabbit hole that can swallow a CEO's time and energy while the real work of leadership is left undone. A great CEO doesn't solve every problem or fight every battle; they know which fires to leave for others to extinguish. The truth is, knowing where *not* to focus isn't a dereliction of duty—it's the essence of strategic leadership.

First, avoid the siren call of routine customer interactions. It might feel noble to jump on every call or respond personally to every issue, but this approach spreads you too thin and undercuts the organization's ability to function independently. Your role is to lead, not to manage the day-to-day grind.

Similarly, steer clear of transactional communications. Order updates, billing disputes, and operational questions are important, but they're not *your* job. If you're finding yourself knee-deep in these issues too often, it's a sign that your team needs more autonomy—or better systems. A CEO's involvement in these areas doesn't project strength or accessibility; it sends a message that the organization isn't equipped to handle the basics without you.

That's a problem for the business and a waste of your time.

A common problem I see is when CEOs slip down the slippery slope of micromanaging customer teams. Trust is the backbone of leadership, and that includes trusting the people you've hired to engage with customers. If you're stepping into day-to-day strategies and second-guessing their every move, you're not just misusing your time—you're undermining theirs. Step in when a higher-level intervention is necessary, but otherwise, give them room to operate and succeed.

Ultimately, the CEO's role in customer relationships is to focus on the big moves: the strategic partnerships, the cultural shifts, the moments that require their unique presence and authority. Wading into the weeds doesn't just dilute your effectiveness—it sends the wrong signal to your team. Great CEOs know when to say no, not out of neglect but out of respect for the bigger picture. Their time is their most valuable asset, and how they choose to spend it—or not spend it—defines the culture and future of their company.

HOW TO BEST INTERACT WITH CUSTOMERS

When a CEO steps into a room with a key customer, it's not just another meeting—it's an opportunity to craft a moment that will stay with them long after you leave. Think of it like Eddie Vedder stepping on stage. The Pearl Jam frontman has a ritual: He keeps track of the setlists he's played in each city so he never repeats the same show. He respects the audience enough to bring something fresh, something uniquely tailored for them. CEOs need that same respect for their customers. Each interaction should feel custom-made, a reflection of the customer's industry, culture, and personal preferences. You're not there to deliver a generic pitch—you're there to deliver an experience.

Memorability is the currency of a CEO's time with customers. Yes, that's a lot of pressure. But so what? That's what you're paid for. Every moment you spend with a client is a chance to tell a story about your company, a story that roots your culture in their mind. Not a story about the BMW you just bought or the game-winning shot you made in high school, unless—and this is crucial—those anecdotes are a vehicle to a larger point about your company's values or vision. Your personal charm can entertain, but it won't stick unless it's tied to something bigger. The goal is to have customers walking away saying, "I *get* what this company is about."

Leave the hard sell to your sales team. If you're in the weeds explaining features and benefits, you've missed the point. That's not your job as the CEO. If your business depends on you doing that, it's a sign you haven't built a scalable operation. Your role is to elevate the conversation—to zoom out and show customers the bigger picture of your company's mission and culture. You're there to make them feel like insiders, like partners in something bigger than a transaction.

Tailor every interaction with intention. Before you meet, take the time to understand who they are and what they value. Are they more numbers-driven or narrative-driven? Do they prefer directness, or is a softer approach more appropriate? Customers notice when you've done your homework, and they appreciate it when you meet them on their terms. Your ability to adjust your style to fit their needs shows respect and builds trust.

Ultimately, every interaction is an investment in the relationship. Just as Eddie Vedder never phones it in, you can't either. Treat each meeting as if it's the only chance you'll have to make an impression—because, in many cases, it might be. Respect the customer, respect their time, and make it count.

No matter how charismatic or tireless a CEO might be, the reality is stark: Customer relationships can't depend on one person. Beware of bottlenecking! The real magic of a CEO's involvement isn't in being indispensable but in setting up systems that make the company indispensable. A CEO should think like an architect, designing a framework where every customer interaction carries the same thoughtfulness and care, whether it's with a junior associate or the CEO themself. The goal isn't just customer satisfaction—it's institutionalizing a culture where customers feel like partners in something bigger.

Here's how you can do that:

INSTITUTIONALIZING FEEDBACK LOOPS

The best CEOs aren't just listening to customers—they're taking notes, connecting dots, and building a map. Where I see some failing is when they fall into the trap: believing their own BS. I've lost count of the number of companies that confidently proclaim, "We have the *best* customer service in the industry!" Okay, but what's the benchmark? Are you measuring against actual customer feedback, or is it just the echo chamber of your executive team? You can't afford to lie to yourself here. Set up formal systems to collect insights from customers—real, unvarnished feedback. Every time you're in a room with a customer, think of it as reconnaissance. Your job is to bring those insights back, not to hoard them as anecdotes for your next cocktail party, but to feed them into systems that translate them into action.

You can't just ask for feedback; show customers what you've done with it. That's the difference between a company that listens and one that evolves. Feedback loops shouldn't just be operational—they should be transformational, turning customer insights into better products, better service, and a stronger culture.

Developing Customer Advocacy Programs

Here's a secret: Your best customers want to do more than buy from you—they want to be part of your story. But you have to ask. The savviest CEOs enlist their top customers as brand ambassadors, advisory board members, or even informal coaches for the company. These shouldn't be seen as vanity titles but as strategic roles in shaping your product and services. A customer who feels invested in your success will work harder for your brand than any marketing team ever could.

Think of it like a championship team. The fans who paint their faces and memorize stats aren't just fans—they're fanatics. They feel ownership. By inviting customers into your inner circle, you're turning passive buyers into active participants, deepening their connection while leveraging their influence.

Scaling the CEO's Impact

The common mistake CEOs make is thinking they need to personally handle every major customer. That's not scalable, and more importantly, it's not necessary. Your role is to set the tone and create the culture, then put systems in place to make sure that culture permeates every corner of the organization.

Create mechanisms for sharing customer insights broadly. Make it impossible for anyone in the company to forget the importance of the customer, whether they're on the sales floor or in the back office. Build rituals, like sharing customer stories in team meetings, that keep relationships at the forefront. A culture that values customers doesn't happen by accident—it happens because the CEO demands it, builds systems to sustain it, and refuses to let it be an afterthought.

Ultimately, the CEO's job isn't to be everywhere at once. It's to ensure that every customer interaction, at every level, carries the fingerprints of the culture they've worked so hard to create.

Great companies aren't built on products or even profits—they're built on relationships. And no one has more power to shape those relationships than the CEO. This isn't about being a hero or a savior; it's about being a leader. It's about showing your team—and your customers—that the company stands for something bigger than itself. When a CEO prioritizes customer relationships, they aren't just building loyalty or boosting sales; they're creating a culture, a legacy.

As we've explored, the relationship a CEO cultivates with their customers is a cornerstone of a thriving business—rooted in empathy, authenticity, and strategic focus.

But even the strongest external relationships hinge on the foundation of an internal one: the relationship a CEO has with themself. After all, a leader's ability to connect, inspire, and build trust with others is directly tied to their own clarity, self-awareness, and resilience. In the next chapter, we'll dive into what is arguably the most critical relationship of all—how a CEO manages their own mindset, energy, and well-being to lead with purpose and vision. Because without investing in *yourself*, it's impossible to truly invest in others.

QUICK RELATIONSHIP AUDIT

Ask yourself:

- Have you personally connected with your top customers this quarter?
- Can you name your top revenue and referral-generating clients?
- Do your customers know what your company stands for?

- Have you created systems to capture and act on customer feedback?
- Do your employees see you model customer-first behavior?

Chapter 6

YOURSELF

Ben Horowitz sat in his office in 2001, staring at the ceiling as though it might offer a way out. Loudcloud, the company he had co-founded, was hemorrhaging cash faster than it could raise new funding. The market had turned against him. The dot-com bubble had burst, and every VC in Silicon Valley who had eagerly written checks just months earlier was now nowhere to be found. "You have to get through this," he told himself, his mind racing. "But how?"

If anyone understood the demands of being a CEO, it was Ben Horowitz. He would later joke, "By the time we took Loudcloud public, I was so stressed out, I thought the underwriters might have to carry me onto the stage." But beneath the humor was a stark truth: His ability to manage his own well-being was directly tied to his ability to lead. The survival of his company, the livelihoods of his employees, and the outcomes of every high-stakes decision were all tethered to the mental clarity, resilience, and energy he could bring to the table.

Horowitz wasn't new to pressure. Years earlier, he had been a rising star at Netscape, learning how to build a company from the ground up. But nothing in his career could have prepared him for the sheer volume and intensity of demands that came with being the CEO of a startup on the brink. He was, as he described it, "the lonely CEO"—the one everyone looks to for answers, even when you have none.

For Horowitz, stress wasn't just an abstract idea; it was a physical and psychological force with real consequences. The relentless pace of decision-making, the emotional toll of carrying a company's fate on his shoulders, and the isolation of leadership began to chip away at him. "As a startup CEO, I slept like a baby," he once quipped. "I woke up every two hours and cried."

Eventually, he came to see that managing his own well-being wasn't separate from his role—it was central to it. He reframed self-care not as a personal indulgence but as a leadership discipline. Stress couldn't be eliminated, but it could be managed. He found outlets—like his love for hip-hop music, which helped him channel emotion and stay grounded. He worked out. He leaned on trusted advisors. He carved out space to reflect.

By the time Loudcloud evolved into Opsware and was sold to HP for $1.6 billion, Horowitz had learned a lesson every CEO must confront: If you don't manage yourself, you're no good to anyone else. Not your board. Not your team. Not your company.

Ben Horowitz's journey underscores a reality every CEO must face: The greatest threat to a company's long-term success isn't always the competition, market shifts, or capital—it's the leader's own ability to stay clear, grounded, and resilient. Every external relationship—bosses, team, collaborators, community, customers—depends first on the internal one: the relationship you have with yourself. This chapter is about that relationship.

How this chapter works: We'll start with the *inner work*—the habits that create clarity and focus (journaling, self-talk, and personal goal setting). Then we'll move to *personal development*—your ongoing learning and growth (mental health first, then physical health, reading, and what I call *exposure to genius*). Finally, we'll anchor it in *personal relationships*—family, friends, and a trusted circle—because the people outside the office keep the leader inside the office whole.

THE INNER WORK

The inner work of leadership isn't as visible as board presentations or client dinners, but it is no less essential. You are the most important asset of your company. If you break down, every other relationship in the business eventually suffers. On the other side of that coin, if you can create internal clarity and focus, you and your company will have access to a superpower.

Managing yourself is an "inside job," this is a responsibility that you cannot delegate or outsource. Yes, there are some people who can help you, which we will explore later in this chapter, but the real benefits come from the work you are willing to put in yourself.

Inner work begins with carving out space. White space on your calendar. Reflection before your day begins. Time to think without interruption. These habits are not to be seen as luxuries but as leadership disciplines. As a CEO, you operate in a storm of distraction. The real danger isn't missing an email; it's losing the ability to distinguish the urgent from the truly important. It's about controlling your focus.

In my time as a CEO, coach, and board member, I've tested dozens of approaches to this inner work. A few rise above the rest. They aren't complicated, but they require commitment and discipline and most importantly, a willingness to just begin. In my experience, three practices consistently deliver outsized returns: journaling, managing your self-talk, and personal goal setting.

By working on these three things, you can get to know yourself and thrive. Let's take a look at the first tool: journaling.

JOURNALING

Journaling has been one of my life's secret weapons. I've kept journals for more than two decades. Writing helps me think more clearly, unload emotional baggage, and find patterns in the chaos. I have talked to individuals and groups about journaling and so many people have come back to me to tell me how their journals have helped them think clearer and be more present.

The Roman emperor Marcus Aurelius wrote *Meditations* not for an audience but for himself, to wrestle with doubt, sharpen his thinking, and stay grounded under the weight of empire. CEOs today can do the same.

Journaling creates clarity and a record of learning and emotional processing. Starting with just one line a day—*What mattered most today?*—is enough. Over time, patterns appear. You begin to see what drives you, drains you, and repeats itself.

How do you begin journaling? Just start. Write down what's bothering you, what energized you today, what you're grateful for, or who you need to reconnect with. Don't worry about making it perfect. You don't need a fancy app; a regular lined notebook or a blank page on a Google Doc is a great way to begin. Just get it down.

Over my years of journaling and trials and errors, I have developed some habits that have benefitted me and my practice:

- **Pen and Paper.** There is something powerful about putting pen to paper and letting thoughts travel from your mind through your hand onto a page. Yes, typing or dictating works, but handwriting carries a kind of transference that feels deeper and more permanent. I've kept Moleskine notebooks for years, rotating between red and black, and I use the same pens over and over (a black Uni Vision Elite or blue Pilot Neo-Gel). Familiarity with these tools helps anchor the practice.

- **Gratitude Practice.** Each day, I write down three things I'm grateful for. My rule: They must be specific and nonrepetitive. I try to capture something from the last twenty-four hours—small moments, personal interactions, or unique experiences. Gratitude crowds out fear; it's nearly impossible to feel both at once.

- **Create Lists.** Journals don't need to be filled with essays. Lists work just as well. I keep sections for favorites: best meals of the year, shows or movies I enjoyed watching, cool places I visited, people I was glad to see. These lists are fun, but they also create an inventory of joy.

- **Audience of One.** I remind myself that I am the only audience for my journals. They're not meant to impress anyone, they're simply a place to be honest.
- **Reflection.** While I don't reread everything, I regularly go back. It's humbling and often surprising to see what I once worried about, or to rediscover insights I'd forgotten.

Journaling helps you clear mental clutter. And over time, it gives you a track record and written proof of your own growth. But journaling is not the only place where your thoughts and ideas go to live; in fact, most of your thoughts and ideas are constantly bouncing around your head in the form of self-talk. We are always talking to ourselves. Awareness of this ongoing conversation and working to manage this is key to your well-being. Let's explore how managing your self-talk can be used for growth and improving your personal relationship.

SELF-TALK

Self-talk is the soundtrack running through every leader's mind. Most of the time, we don't even notice it—it's automatic. But peak performers train it. Dr. Michael Gervais, one of the world's leading performance psychologists, emphasizes that awareness of self-talk is the first step. You can't upgrade the dialogue in your head if you don't even hear it.

Once you notice it, the work is in the reframing. Negative self-talk—"I'm not ready" or "I can't handle this"—narrows your perspective and triggers fear. Constructive self-talk widens it: "I've faced harder before." "What's the lesson here?" This isn't about blind optimism. It's the deliberate choice to speak to yourself as a coach rather than a critic.

In my years of leading and working with individuals and listening to countless interviews of peak performers in all walks of life, I have observed a consistent pattern: The most successful people almost always narrate their lives in ways that empower them. They see events as unfolding *for them*—opportunities to learn, grow, and move forward. In contrast, people who stay stuck often frame themselves as victims, seeing every setback as something done *to them*. The difference isn't circumstance but the narrative they choose to tell. And that narrative is just another form of self-talk.

Like any skill, empowering self-talk requires reps. That's why you need to learn and build tools that will help you build daily awareness and repetition. Over time, the practice compounds. Self-talk shifts from being a liability to becoming one of your greatest assets.

When it comes to my own self-talk, I've found two practices especially powerful:

My Morning Mantra. I start each day by telling myself, "Today is your best friend." This simple line centers me and pulls me into the present. If I'm carrying regrets from yesterday, it reminds me that today is the day I can act differently. If I'm anxious about the future, it grounds me in the truth that tomorrow only improves through what I do today. Above all else, it reminds me that all I truly have is today—and that living deliberately, one day at a time, is where progress and peace come from.

The Three Conversations. I use runs and walks as times to direct my self-talk toward three different versions of myself: the eight-year-old, the eighteen-year-old, and the eighty-year-old me. Each brings a different perspective.

- **The eight-year-old Eddy** is wide-eyed and joyful, reminding me to be present, to enjoy being outdoors, and to cherish family and friends. He doesn't understand why I'd waste energy on grudges or petty conflicts.
- **The eighteen-year-old Eddy** is ambitious and hungry, urging me to chase big goals. But he's also naive, and I know to temper his drive with perspective. I tell this version how far we've come and the obstacles we faced to get here. I don't want to let him down.
- **The eighty-year-old Eddy** looks back, hoping to see that I took care of the people I loved, did the right thing when it was hard, and

pursued my goals with intention and grit. Above all, this version reminds me of how precious time is and how I need to make the most of what I have in the present.

These conversations give me a kind of internal board of directors. They help me find my center, clarify what really matters, and ensure that the voice in my head pushes me toward the best version of myself. These practices work for me, but the larger point is that every CEO needs to find their own version of this. Self-talk is either the voice that quietly undermines you or the one that helps you rise to the occasion. By making it intentional—through mantras, structured reflections, or simple habits—you give yourself a tool that keeps you steady, focused, and at your best when the stakes are highest.

The voice in your head is powerful, but it's only part of the equation. To stay grounded as a CEO, you also need clarity about where you're headed. That's where personal goals come in—the compass that keeps you moving in the right direction, no matter how loud the noise around you gets.

PERSONAL GOALS

If self-talk helps you manage the moment, then personal goals help you chart the course. Goals are more than tasks on a checklist; they are a declaration of what you value and where you intend to go. For a CEO, setting personal goals is not separate from leading the company; it is the act of aligning your own growth with the growth of the business.

Too often, leaders treat personal goals as optional, something to consider "if there's time." But neglecting them is a mistake. Without personal goals, you drift. You respond to the fires in front of you instead of shaping the horizon ahead. When you write down goals, you give yourself a compass—something to measure your actions against when the noise of daily leadership threatens to pull you off course.

Think of personal goals as layered:

- **Career.** These go beyond the goals of your company and focus on what *you* want to accomplish as a leader and individual. What skills do you want to build? Are there professional experiences you want outside of your current role? What are your financial needs and long-term expectations—and what concrete steps will get you there?
- **Community.** These goals center on the relationships and communities that matter most. How do you want to show up for your family and friends? What role do you want to play in your community? What joy do you want to create in your life and how will you make time for fun and shared experiences?
- **Character.** These are about your own achievements, fulfillment, and growth. Do you want to write a book? Run a marathon? Deepen your spiritual life or travel to certain places? Hobbies you want to take up or build up skills in? These goals help you articulate the life you want beyond business and relationships.

Business goals are public—you share them with your board, your team, your investors. Personal goals, on the other hand, belong to you. That doesn't mean they live only in your head. The act of writing them down transforms them from vague aspirations into commitments. CEOs often underestimate the power of this simple act. A private document, revisited quarterly or annually, can be more powerful than any slide deck.

The true challenge of personal goals is not in setting them but in reviewing them. Revisit them regularly—whether weekly, monthly, or quarterly. Ask yourself: *Am I living in line with these priorities? If not, what's pulling me away?* This reflection is not about guilt; it's about recalibration. Goals should evolve as you evolve. The discipline is in refusing to let them gather dust.

Setting goals gives you a compass, but a compass alone doesn't move you forward—you need to keep growing to reach those destinations. That's why personal development is such an essential part of leading yourself. As CEO, you have a responsibility not just to set goals but to continually invest in your own learning, perspective, and growth.

PERSONAL DEVELOPMENT

Personal development isn't just about classes or certifications. It's about cultivating the whole person: your mental well-being, your physical health, your personal interests, and your ongoing learning. This includes everything from finding hobbies that bring you joy, to building routines that keep you mentally and physically sharp, to engaging with the kinds of ideas and thinkers that expand your worldview.

For CEOs, learning is the lever. Reading widely, pursuing executive education, and deliberately seeking "exposure to genius" are the habits that keep you fresh, relevant, and adaptable in a changing world. But before you push forward—before you sign up for new programs or set ambitious new expectations—you need to pause. Because personal development without a foundation of mental health doesn't stick. If you're running on fumes, the smartest strategies in the world won't matter.

That's why the first and most important dimension of personal development is tending to your mental health.

MENTAL HEALTH

Mental health is the unspoken frontier of CEO leadership. Too many leaders only deal with it after a collapse. Preventive attention is always stronger than crisis management.

Ben Horowitz captured this truth when he said, "By far the most difficult skill I learned as CEO was the ability to manage my own psychology." He didn't mean this as a throwaway line—it was his lifeline. From the outside, running a company looks hard. But from the inside, it's emotionally brutal.

I've seen too many CEOs suffer in silence. They carry stress like armor, afraid that any sign of vulnerability will make them look weak. But the cracks don't disappear just because you hide them—they widen. And eventually, the pressure breaks through.

That's why leaders like Toto Wolff, principal of Mercedes F1, speak so openly about therapy. Wolff has logged more than five hundred hours in sessions, not because he's broken, but because he's committed to peak performance. "Getting help is how I access untapped potential," he says. Seeking professional support is not a sign of weakness—it's a sign of strength.

For CEOs unsure where to start, the first step is simple: ask around. You'll be surprised how many people in your network are open about their own experiences once you break the silence. Building a short list of trusted mental health professionals before you need them is one of the best investments you can make. Even if you don't need a therapist right now, someone close to you might.

Even the highest achievers face these challenges. Michael Phelps—the most decorated Olympian in history—struggled with depression after years of carrying the weight of performance. It wasn't medals that saved him; it was admitting he needed help. His story is a reminder that even the strongest performers benefit from support, not in spite of their success but because of it.

PHYSICAL HEALTH

If mental health is the foundation, your next building block is your physical health. Without it, everything else slows down. This isn't a book about diet hacks or workout plans—you can find endless shelves of that advice elsewhere. The point here is simpler: As a CEO, you owe it to yourself, your company, and your family to take your physical well-being seriously. It's your responsibility.

When I refer to physical health, I'm not just talking about appearance. I am talking about energy, confidence, and performance. The connection between body and mind is undeniable—when you feel strong, you think more clearly. When you're rested, you make better decisions. When you're fit, you lead with more presence. Ignoring your health is not just a personal liability; it's a business one. Here are my thoughts on the keys to building a good physical health program:

- **Find what works for you.** There's no single right formula. For some it's CrossFit, swimming, or Pilates. For others, it's running, lifting, or a Peloton in the home gym. The best routine is the one you'll actually do—the one that makes you feel good and fits your lifestyle. Set goals that make sense for you. Training for an ultra-marathon might be rewarding, but it also comes with trade-offs in work and family life. Be honest about those costs.
- **Make it fun.** The best exercise gives you more than strength or cardio—it gives you energy. I love running, not just for fitness, but because I like to be outside and spend some time alone. For others, it might be pickup basketball, which delivers exercise *and* connection with friends. When you enjoy it, you stick with it—and the benefits multiply.
- **Food as fuel (and joy).** Eat well, but don't overcomplicate it. Nutrition should sustain you, not drain you. And while food fuels performance, it also brings joy. A great meal with friends or colleagues can be as restorative as a workout. Health and happiness aren't mutually exclusive.

Break a sweat every day. Strength, cardio, stretching, walking—any movement counts. Eat responsibly and make good choices when looking at the menu or snack table. Know what healthy looks and feels like for you, and live by it. You don't need to be in constant "beast mode." You just need to be consistent.

Managing your physical health involves seeking medical care. Most CEOs wait for a crisis to see a doctor. Don't be that person. Be proactive. Build a relationship with a physician who knows your history and sees you regularly. Think of it as part of your annual planning cycle.

Dr. Jerome Groopman's *How Doctors Think* opened my eyes to how easily patients can be misdiagnosed or rushed through. You are the quarterback of your healthcare team—advocate for yourself. A few principles I've found helpful:

- Come prepared with two to three key issues.
- Ask, "What else could this be?" to avoid tunnel vision.
- Set the tone with your doctor: "I want to be mindful of your time, but I have a few questions I'd like to walk through."
- Don't accept jargon—ask for plain language.
- Stay current on tests, screenings, and specialists, especially if you have family risk factors.

Proactive health management is about accepting responsibility and staying ahead, so you're not blindsided.

Strong mental health gives you resilience. Strong physical health gives you energy. But resilience and energy alone aren't enough. To keep leading at a high level, you need to keep sharpening yourself. Leadership requires more than stamina—it requires perspective, creativity, and insight. And those don't come automatically. They come from deliberate, ongoing learning.

LEARNING

Unlike company initiatives, nobody is going to hand you a syllabus for your own growth. Your HR department won't knock on your door with a sign-up sheet for a training class in the break room. As a CEO, it's your responsibility to keep learning, broadening your perspective, and exposing yourself to new ideas that can change how you think and lead.

There are countless ways to do this: executive education programs, conferences, mentorship, or hobbies that stretch you outside of work. But in my experience, two practices stand above the rest for their ability to create lasting impact: *reading* and what I call *exposure to genius.* Reading is the most reliable way to compound knowledge, expand your worldview, and challenge your assumptions. Exposure to genius is about deliberately seeking out people, ideas, and experiences that elevate your thinking—getting close to brilliance in whatever form it takes. Together, these two practices ensure you never stop sharpening the edge that leadership demands. Let's take a look at these two practices.

Harry Truman put it best: "Not all readers are leaders, but all leaders are readers." Truman believed that while not everyone who reads becomes a leader, a commitment to reading is essential for all leaders who want to keep growing.

Reading is the ultimate force multiplier. It allows you to absorb a lifetime of insight from someone else's hard-won experience. You don't have to live through every mistake yourself—you can borrow the scars of others. Books are time travel, mentorship, and competitive edge all rolled into one.

Warren Buffett once said the best CEOs should "reserve time for quiet reading and thinking." He doesn't treat reading as leisure. It's not about escaping to a beach novel or killing time on a plane. Reading is part of your job.

My advice is simple: Read far and wide. Follow your curiosity, and don't feel guilty about putting a book down if it isn't resonating. Reading should be both disciplined and enjoyable.

So what should you read? Don't limit yourself to airport bestsellers. Mix it up:

- **Biographies:** to see how others navigated power, failure, and resilience.
- **Psychology:** to understand motivation, behavior, and decision-making.
- **Outside your lane:** history, science, the arts, even parenting, to expand perspective.
- **Business books:** but don't just grab what's trending; ask other CEOs which books truly shaped their thinking.

When you find a book that hits, don't skim it. Mark it up. Write in the margins. Capture key takeaways. Revisit it like a coach reviewing game film. The goal isn't to impress others with book titles at a cocktail party—it's to equip yourself for the battlefield of business.

If books aren't yet a habit for you, that's okay. Try podcasts, lectures, or long-form journalism. But don't confuse consumption with learning. If it isn't changing how you think, it's just noise.

One of the most powerful tools I've discovered to expand my thinking is what I call exposure to genius. Find someone who is operating at the peak of their craft—and go watch them work. It doesn't have to be in your industry. In fact, it's often better if it isn't.

Tour the factory of an innovative manufacturing company. Watch a great chef in a kitchen. Spend an afternoon in a studio while a professional musician records. Witness mastery up close, and you'll start raising your own standards without even realizing it.

You don't need to fly halfway around the world to do this. Genius lives in small places, if you look for it. The key is to get close enough to see the details—the habits, the preparation, the intensity.

I've had the privilege to experience this firsthand. Here are some examples:

- **Teaching.** I recently sat in on a class led by my favorite high school teacher, John Lynskey. Even after decades of teaching the same material, he prepared with meticulous notes and poured himself into the session as if it were his first. For his students, it was. That commitment to excellence—bringing full energy to a moment that felt routine to him—was mastery in action.
- **Sports.** A few years back, I was invited to observe championship head coach Rick Pitino run a basketball practice with his Louisville team. It was two days before Christmas, in a rented gym, a throwaway day by most standards. But Pitino was relentless—teaching, correcting, pushing. It wasn't a performance. It was who he was. That practice recalibrated how I think about attention to detail and living your passion every day, not just on game day.

And the lesson applies directly to CEOs: When you watch how a genius prepares, you notice parallels to running a board meeting, pitching an investor, or leading a team. Mastery is about habits repeated with intensity.

One final tip: Don't just watch—capture what you notice. Jot down details in your journal. Otherwise, the inspiration fades quickly. Documenting what you observe turns exposure into practice. Seek out those moments: art, sports, film, music, teaching—genius leaves clues. Go find them.

Books and brilliant people can sharpen your edge, but they can't hold you steady when the weight of leadership gets heavy. That role belongs to the relationships outside of work—the people who remind you who you are when the title is stripped away.

PERSONAL RELATIONSHIPS

The irony of leadership is that the higher you climb, the easier it is to feel isolated. You're surrounded by people all day, yet true connection can feel out of reach. That's why investing in your personal relationships isn't optional—it's essential. They are your anchor, your mirror, and your safety net when the pressures of the CEO role threaten to consume you.

I think of them in three categories:

- **Family.** These are the people who know you best and love you beyond your role. A healthy family life doesn't just make you happier; it makes you a more grounded leader. Neglect this, and no amount of business success will feel like enough.
- **Friends.** The friendships that endure outside of your professional life give you perspective and joy. They remind you of the person you were before you were "CEO." They bring humor, release, and a sense of belonging that the boardroom cannot provide.
- **Trusted Circle.** These are your peers, coaches, and mentors—the people who challenge your thinking, hold you accountable, and

walk alongside you in your growth. They are not employees, not family, but they occupy a vital space of truth-telling and perspective. Organizations like YPO and EO formalize this, but it can also be a handful of individuals you deliberately cultivate over time.

Your relationships with family, friends, and your trusted circle are not "nice to have." They are part of your responsibility as a leader. Because when you're at your best in these arenas, you bring a fuller, more resilient version of yourself back into the company.

FAMILY

Tom Brady once said, "Life won't always go your way. But when you have people around you who walk through it with you, it doubles the joy and divides the pain." For CEOs, those people aren't your clients or board members. They're the ones who know you without the title—your spouse, partner, kids, parents, siblings. These are the relationships that remind you who you are, not just what you do. And they're also the first to suffer when you're off balance. If you're not investing in them, you're draining your own battery.

What I hear over and over from CEOs is the myth of "quality time." Quality time is just that—a myth. Being with your family is not about grand gestures or perfectly scheduled vacations. It's about presence. Jerry Seinfeld once described it as "garbage time"—the unscripted, low-stakes moments when you're just there. The car rides. The quiet dinners. The walk around the block. That's when real connection happens.

If you're lucky enough to be a parent, you already know there's no greater responsibility or role. This isn't a parenting book, but it would be irresponsible not to acknowledge how central this relationship is. One of the most important things you can do for your kids is to help them understand what you actually do. Not just "Dad's a CEO" or "Mom runs a company." Share the challenges you're facing—not to burden them, but to model what hard work, leadership, and problem-solving look like. Those conversations shape how they see ambition, responsibility, and purpose.

And don't fall into the trap of believing that missed moments can be made up with big vacations or expensive trips. Your kids don't need Disney or Italy—they need you in the everyday. On the drive to school. On the sidelines at practice. At the dinner table without your phone. Garbage time is where the good stuff happens, and you have to be there for it.

Finally, one of the most powerful checks on your own well-being is simple: Ask your partner how you're showing up at home. Not how often—*how present.* You may not love the answer, but you'll need it.

FRIENDS

If family grounds you, friends keep you human. They're the people who remind you that life isn't just about quarterly earnings or new product development—it's also about laughing until your stomach hurts, repeating the same inside jokes, swapping old stories, and being there for one another through the ups and downs.

But friendships at the CEO level can be tricky. Busy schedules make it easy to neglect them. The danger is believing you can put these relationships on hold until "things slow down." They rarely do. And friendships, unlike business, can't always be revived on demand.

Friendship isn't about poker night or an annual golf trip, though those can be fun. Friendship is about showing up. Call your friends when you sense they might need a few minutes to talk. Celebrate their victories—no matter how small. And always go to the funerals of their loved ones. Your presence in both joy and grief matters more than any text or email ever could.

There are practical ways to keep friendships alive even with a packed schedule. For years, I have had to travel often for business. I keep a list of friends in the cities I visit and I schedule time to see them while I'm in town. Old colleagues, college buddies, people you've lost touch with—schedule a dinner, coffee, or drinks the next time you're passing through. Keep that running list. For your friends who live in your city, commit to a rhythm: a monthly lunch, a quarterly dinner. Small rituals keep the bonds strong.

The throughline is simple: Don't neglect your friends. They are the ones who will keep you honest, make you laugh, and remind you that leadership is only one part of a much larger life.

TRUSTED CIRCLE

Family and friends nurture your heart, but CEOs also need a circle that sharpens the mind and spirit. This is your *trusted circle*—the peers, mentors, and coaches who are there for *you,* not your company. They're not on the company payroll. They're not there for a transaction. They're invested in your well-being, your growth, and your clarity as a leader and as a human being.

This circle doesn't happen by accident. It's on you, as the CEO, to build it. That might mean formal organizations like YPO, EO, or Hampton, where structure and confidentiality create space for vulnerability. Or it could be a handful of trusted advisors you've cultivated over time—people who tell you the truth when others won't, who challenge your thinking, and who give you perspective when the noise gets too loud.

A good trusted circle blends three roles:

- **Peers** who understand the challenges because they live them too.
- **Mentors** who've walked the path ahead of you and can share lessons learned.
- **Coaches** who push you, hold you accountable, and keep you aligned with your best self.

Whatever form it takes, the goal is the same: to surround yourself with people who won't let you settle, who see you not as a CEO but as a leader-in-progress. The higher you climb, the lonelier it gets—unless you deliberately build the relationships that keep you grounded.

Family, friends, and a trusted circle are not "extras" to squeeze in when your calendar allows. They're part of the infrastructure that makes everything else possible. They steady you when life goes sideways, keep you grounded when success inflates your ego, and remind you that you are more than your role. Nurturing these relationships doesn't take time away from leadership—it strengthens it.

Your inner work, your mental health, your physical well-being, your ongoing development, and your personal relationships all add up to one truth: *You are the company's most important asset.* If you fail to manage yourself, everything else eventually crumbles.

Arthur Brooks captured it perfectly: "Your life is the most important management task you will ever undertake."

So treat it that way. Lead yourself with the same intentionality you bring to your board, your team, your customers, and your community. Because when you are clear, strong, and grounded, every other relationship flourishes.

FROM ARENAS TO EXECUTION

The six arenas of relationships define the world a CEO must master. But awareness alone isn't enough. The question now becomes: How do you act on it?

In the next section, we'll move from arenas to execution. I'll introduce the CARPE framework—a system for making relationships intentional, durable, and transformative. As always, we'll draw lessons from business, culture, and history, alongside stories from my own experience as a CEO, board member, and coach. The focus now shifts from *what* to *how.*

That's where a framework comes in. A framework is a tool for mastery. It keeps you from treating relationships as improvisation or personality-driven charm. It turns the art of relationships into a repeatable system. CARPE is not about "being nice" or "networking harder." It's about bringing discipline, focus, and strategy to the most human part of leadership.

The name is intentional. *Carpe diem* means "seize the day." CARPE means "seize the tool." This framework is your call to action. It's not enough to understand that relationships matter. You must seize them, shape them, and use them to drive outcomes. CARPE gives you the lens to do that.

Think of it as a decision filter. Every day as a CEO, you face dozens of moments where relationships could be leveraged, strengthened, or repaired. CARPE gives you a way to pause and ask: *Am I connecting? Are we aligned? How should I respond? What do I need to prioritize? How do I evaluate this?*

Used consistently, CARPE becomes second nature—a habit of relational leadership.

Here's the framework in plain terms:

- **Connect.** Relationships begin with connection. This isn't about networking—it's about being present, curious, and intentional in building trust. Connection is the spark that makes everything else possible.
- **Align.** Great leaders align people around shared goals, even when interests or egos conflict. Alignment transforms connection into momentum.
- **Respond.** Leaders are judged by how they respond in moments of stress and uncertainty. Responding well means staying grounded, listening first, and choosing actions that build trust rather than erode it.
- **Prioritize.** Not every relationship deserves equal time or energy. Prioritization means knowing who matters most right now and investing accordingly.
- **Evaluate.** Relationships are dynamic. Evaluating means regularly stepping back and asking what's working, what's not, and where adjustments are needed.

Together, these moves form a system. Each is powerful on its own, but it's the combination that creates mastery.

Think of CARPE as both a framework and a lens. It gives you language to teach your team, a structure to map in workshops, and a filter for daily decisions. When faced with a conflict, a new opportunity, or a shifting power dynamic, CARPE gives you a way to think: *Am I missing a step here? Do I need to reconnect? Realign? Reprioritize?*

It is both art and science—practical enough to use in a board meeting, but human enough to shape how you show up with your family at dinner.

Connection is where it all starts. You can't align, respond, prioritize, or evaluate without first establishing a real bond. That's the first move of CARPE—and it may be the most essential. In the next chapter, we'll dive deep into what it means to *connect* as a leader, and why it's the key that unlocks every other part of relational leadership strategy.

QUICK RELATIONSHIPS AUDIT

Ask yourself:

- Do I consistently make time for reflection and focus?
- Do I have a plan for my physical and mental health?
- Am I investing in learning and personal growth?
- Who are the key people who keep me grounded—and am I nurturing those relationships?

KEY TAKEAWAYS

- **You are the company's greatest asset.** If you don't manage yourself well—physically, mentally, and emotionally—everything else begins to crumble.
- **Inner work builds clarity.** Taking the time for reflection helps build resilience and leads to better judgment.
- **Your growth is your responsibility.** Reading, reflection, and exposure to new ideas are how you stay sharp and adapt to a fast-moving world.
- **Success without self-awareness is dangerous.** Define your personal values and build habits that align with who you are and what you truly want.

PART II

THE CARPE FRAMEWORK

<u>**Chapter 7**</u>

CONNECT

On May 1, 1969, the air in the Senate chamber was heavy with impatience. Senator John Pastore sat elevated above the witness table, his reputation as a budget hawk on full display. He had already spent the morning grilling witnesses, slicing through charts and policy statements with the irritation of a man convinced that every extra dollar for public programs was one dollar wasted. Pastore was blunt, dismissive, even bored. The witnesses looked nervous. They should have. Nixon's administration had proposed cutting public broadcasting in half—$20 million down to $10 million—and Pastore was eager to oblige.

And then, into this arena, walked Fred Rogers.

He didn't look like a man who could save a national institution. He was soft-spoken, slight, with his wire-rimmed glasses and his gentle Pittsburgh cadence. No entourage. No towering presence. No prepared slide presentation. Just a stack of notes he would never actually read.

If Pastore swung a hammer, Rogers struck a tuning fork. He didn't meet the senator with bluster or technical arguments. Instead, he spoke about children—about what it meant to give them a space where their feelings were acknowledged, where they could learn to manage anger and fear without violence. His tone never rose above conversational. He recited, from memory, the words of one of his own scripts, about trusting yourself when the world feels overwhelming.

The chamber went still. For a moment, it didn't feel like a Senate hearing at all. It felt like one man speaking directly to another, human to human.

Pastore leaned back. The corner of his mouth twitched. "I think it's wonderful," he said, almost grudgingly. Then, after a pause that carried the weight of $20 million: "Looks like you just earned the money."

Rogers had done in six minutes what battalions of lobbyists and policy experts couldn't. He hadn't fought. He hadn't argued. He had connected.

What Rogers did in Washington was dramatic, but it wasn't unique. His gift was the same whether he was in a Senate chamber or a child's bedroom, broadcast through the television screen. Consider the story of a young boy with cerebral palsy who had written to Rogers. The boy couldn't travel, so Rogers went to him. The family expected a quick handshake or maybe a photograph. Instead, Rogers stayed for hours, sitting by the boy's bed, listening, singing, asking questions. When the boy became frustrated with his limitations, Rogers leaned closer and asked him to pray for *him*. The mother later said it was the first time her son had believed he had something to give.

That was the genius of Fred Rogers. He didn't merely entertain or reassure. He collapsed the distance between himself and the person in front of him, whether a senator guarding the federal budget or a boy in a hospital bed. He made people feel not just heard, but needed.

This chapter—and each of the chapters that follow in the CARPE framework—follows a rhythm. We'll start by making the case for why this step matters, then move into *how* to practice it: tools, tactics, and exercises you can use to strengthen your own leadership. Along the way, I'll share examples not only from business and culture, but also from my own experience as a CEO and as a coach working with leaders. We'll also look at the common obstacles that can get in the way, and how to avoid them. And finally, each chapter will close with a quick "relationship audit" and key takeaways you can apply immediately. The goal isn't just understanding the framework—it's practicing it.

WHY CONNECTING MATTERS

For CEOs, connection is the starting line. Without it, nothing else in leadership works. Alignment falters. Responses are misinterpreted. Priorities drift. Evaluations become empty. Connection is the condition for all the rest.

Connection builds trust faster than any title or résumé. It cuts through skepticism and noise, giving your words weight because people feel you mean them. It also creates clarity—misunderstandings shrink when people feel safe enough to ask questions and share doubts. And perhaps most overlooked: Connection creates energy. People will work harder and endure more if they feel their leader is *with* them, not above them.

Yet connection is often dismissed as "soft." Many leaders assume their title or intelligence is enough to win loyalty. It isn't. Leadership isn't about commanding attention, but about creating resonance. People follow leaders who make them feel seen.

Connection doesn't require charisma. Rogers wasn't charismatic in the traditional sense. He was quiet, unpolished, even awkward at times. But his presence created safety. His consistency built trust. His curiosity about people made them open up.

We picture CEOs as masters of projection—big voices, big visions— but the real power lies in attunement: tuning yourself to others so they feel seen. It's about closing the gap between you and the people who matter most—your board, your team, your customers, your community.

That's why *connect* is the first step in the CARPE framework. Before you can align, respond, prioritize, or evaluate, you need to create the condition that allows people to lean in. Rogers proved it in a Senate chamber. CEOs must prove it every day in boardrooms, town halls, and one-on-ones. Seize the chance to connect, and everything else follows.

Understanding why connection matters is only part of the task. The harder—and more rewarding—work is figuring out how to actually do it in the chaos of daily leadership. Connection doesn't happen by accident. It comes from building habits, using tools, and making deliberate choices about how you show up for others.

In the next section, we'll look at practical ways to practice connection. I'll share examples from my own experience as a CEO and coach, highlight research-backed approaches, and draw lessons from leaders in business, sports, and culture. These aren't abstract ideas—they're tactics you can start applying today to shrink the distance between you and the people who matter most in your organization.

HOW TO PRACTICE IT: TOOLS AND TACTICS

Connection isn't luck, and it isn't charm; it's the practice of initiating relationships with purpose and authenticity. A practice you build, refine, and repeat until it becomes a way of being. The most effective leaders don't just *have it*; they work at it. They prepare before the meeting, they listen differently during the meeting, and they follow up after the meeting in ways that deepen the bond. Over time, those habits compound into trust, loyalty, and influence.

In this section, we'll explore three tools that make connection tangible. Each is a discipline you can learn and apply, whether you're leading a board meeting, negotiating a deal, or having a one-on-one with a direct report:

- **Finding the Thread:** discovering the deeper story or value that makes another person lean in.
- **Build the Bridge:** creating familiarity and trust when you don't yet have a relationship, by leaning on shared ground and trusted connections.
- **Marking the Moments:** meeting people at the points of celebration and humanity that matter most to them.

Connection, like any discipline, begins with awareness. Before you can build or bridge, you have to *see* what truly connects people—the detail, the value, or the emotion that matters most to them. The first tool is about developing that instinct. It's learning to look past titles and transactions and instead listen for the signal that turns a conversation into a relationship.

FINDING THE THREAD

Every meaningful connection starts with a thread. It's not always obvious. Sometimes it's buried beneath numbers, negotiations, or small talk. But if you can find it—the value, story, or motivation that matters most to the other person—you unlock the doorway to trust.

I learned this firsthand during one of the most pivotal moments in building Apollo Bank.

We were pursuing the acquisition of a competitor bank that seemed like a perfect fit: the right geography, the right customer base, and the kind of platform that could accelerate our growth. But the odds weren't in our favor. Bigger competitors with deeper pockets were circling, and if it came down to a bidding war, we'd be outgunned. To make matters more complicated, we didn't yet have the funding fully secured—we'd have to raise capital after signing the deal. We were the challenger, not the favorite.

At first, my team and I did what everyone does in situations like this: We built the pitch. We polished a deck, stacked the financials, and rehearsed the talking points. That's what you're supposed to do. But the more I studied the seller—let's call him Mr. P—the more I realized the standard playbook wouldn't work.

Mr. P wasn't selling because he needed the money. His family had been in banking for literally centuries, with businesses spread across the globe. He was already wealthy. This was about something deeper—legacy, pride, and ensuring the bank's people and community would be cared for.

If I went in with our story or a set of financial arguments, I'd be just another bidder. What mattered wasn't the story of *us*, but the story of *him*. How he came into the family legacy, what it meant to him, how he saw his role as custodian of a tradition.

So we scrapped the deck.

When we sat down with Mr. P, I asked about all the other businesses he was involved in, about the history of his family in banking, about the lessons he carried from his grandfather. I let him tell the story he clearly wanted to tell. I listened. And when it was my turn, we didn't roll out a flashy proposal. We laid out three plain, simple deal points—face-to-face, no slides, no showmanship.

That night, I wrote him a handwritten note. I thanked him for sharing his story and pointed to the details that had struck me: the pride he carried, the way he talked about his employees, the responsibility he felt to protect a legacy. I wanted him to know I had actually heard him. Early the next morning, before his flight, I had the note delivered to his penthouse apartment.

A week later, his attorney called. "Mr. P received your note," he said. "I don't know what you wrote, but he told me you reminded him of how his grandfather used to do business. You should also know: You were the only bidder who didn't submit a formal written proposal. And you were the lowest bidder. But Mr. P wants to give you a thirty-day exclusive."

We signed the deal. We raised the capital. And Mr. P became not only a client but a long-term supporter.

That's the power of finding the thread.

How to Apply

- **Ask before you tell.** Instead of opening with your story, invite them to share theirs.
- **Look for the thread.** Listen for what matters most: legacy, loyalty, pride, vision. These are usually the deeper drivers beneath the surface.

- **Weave it back.** Reflect what you've heard—in your conversation, in your follow-up, or in the way you shape your proposal.
- **Make it personal.** A handwritten note, a thoughtful gesture, or a simple acknowledgment often carries more weight than polished presentations.
- **Keep it simple.** Don't overcomplicate. Authenticity wins where flash fails.

Connecting with someone you already have a solid relationship with or an open door makes it easier to find the thread, but sometimes you don't have the luxury of sitting across from someone and hearing their story. Sometimes the person is a regulator, a distant shareholder, or an executive at a critical supplier—someone you don't know yet, but whose relationship with you matters. In those cases, connection isn't automatic. You have to build a bridge.

BUILD THE BRIDGE

Bridges get built in small, intentional steps. You start by finding the shared ground you *do* have, even if it's indirect. That might mean reaching through a trusted mutual contact, leaning on shared institutions (like alumni groups, trade associations, or nonprofits), or even just referencing something meaningful you've noticed about them. The point isn't to impress—it's to shorten the distance so the first conversation feels less like strangers talking and more like colleagues beginning a relationship.

Reid Hoffman, the founder of LinkedIn, put it well: "Your network is the people who want to help you, and you want to help them, and that's really powerful." The most reliable way to build that kind of network isn't by cold outreach—it's by tapping into the trust you've already earned. Ask someone who knows you well to make the introduction. When a bridge is built on borrowed trust, the first steps across feel natural, not forced.

Some bridges are built with small gestures: sending an article that relates to a speech they gave, showing up to an event that matters to them, or offering a thoughtful perspective on a challenge they've spoken about publicly. Others require persistence—reaching out more than once, each time adding value instead of just asking for time.

What matters most is intent. If the other person senses you're angling only for access or advantage, the bridge collapses before you've set the first stone. But if they feel your effort is grounded in respect, curiosity, or a genuine desire to understand, you give them reason to step toward you.

How to Apply

- **Leverage warm introductions.** Ask a trusted mutual contact to broker the first conversation. A warm introduction transfers trust and sets the tone.
- **Anchor to shared ground.** If you don't have a mutual contact, look for institutions or experiences you share—a school, a trade group, a board, even a hometown. Start there.
- **Make the first move thoughtful.** Skip the generic LinkedIn note or email blast. Instead, reference something specific about their work or priorities that shows you've done the homework.
- **Follow up with presence.** The bridge doesn't hold after one crossing. Follow up with a gesture—an article relevant to their interest, a short note, or even a quick call to thank them for their time.

Building the bridge isn't about forcing instant intimacy—it's about creating enough familiarity to earn a second conversation. Once that bridge is in place, you can walk across and do the deeper work of finding the thread and continuing to build on the relationship. One way to build on that relationship and connect is by marking the moments that are uniquely significant to the person you are building the relationship with.

When Gregg Popovich announced his retirement from the San Antonio Spurs, the room filled with familiar faces. Former assistants. Retired players. Staff who had been with him for decades. Many had traveled back to San Antonio for the occasion, eager to honor the man who had led them through championships, heartbreaks, and countless team dinners.

Among them was Dejounte Murray. By then, Murray wasn't a Spur anymore. He was playing for the New Orleans Pelicans, his career having moved on. No one would have blinked if he'd stayed away. He didn't owe the franchise—or Popovich—anything. And yet, there he was, seated quietly among the crowd, showing up when it mattered.

The gesture might have seemed small compared to a lifetime of basketball, but it carried a weight. Because Murray hadn't just learned to play under Popovich. He had learned what it meant to show up for people.

Years earlier, when Murray was still a rookie, his mother had been shot back home in Seattle. It was the kind of crisis that could derail a young player before his career had even begun. Popovich stepped in—not with a lecture about focus, not with a stern reminder of professionalism. He picked up the phone, called Murray's mother, and offered to move her to San Antonio, covering the costs himself if necessary. More than that, he let Murray grieve. He listened when the young guard broke down in his office, shoulders shaking. He was a coach, yes, but in those moments he was something closer to a father.

Popovich built his career on that kind of presence. He wasn't just there for the trophies or the big speeches. He showed up in quiet ways—meeting his team at the airport after long road trips, no matter the hour. Knocking on Manu Ginóbili's door at 1:00 a.m. with a bottle of wine after a crushing loss. Gathering the locker room for dinner after Ray Allen's legendary shot in the 2013 Finals, reminding them: "We win together. We lose together. Man's got to eat."

That consistency left a mark. It told players: You are more than your stat line, more than a contract, more than a piece in the Spurs machine. You are human, and I'll be here for you in the moments that matter.

So when the day came for Popovich to step away, Murray didn't send a text or post a highlight reel on Instagram. He showed up. Not because it was good PR. Not because anyone would notice. But because Popovich had shown him how. The relationship had stretched beyond the game, beyond transactions, beyond titles. It was about honoring the thread between them—one woven not in championships, but in presence.

That is what it means to mark the moments. You don't need grand speeches or orchestrated gestures. You need to show up—consistently, authentically, and especially when it matters most.

Popovich's relationship with Murray shows us what it looks like to show up in life's defining moments—a retirement, a crisis, a turning point. But marking the moments doesn't have to wait for the big stage. In fact, the strongest relationships are often built in the smaller touchpoints, the ones that prove you're paying attention when no one else is.

It's not just birthdays or anniversaries. It's remembering the day of a client's big presentation and sending a note of encouragement. It's congratulating a colleague when their child graduates high school, or offering a word of empathy when you hear about a loss in their family. It's noting the good news and the bad news, and letting them know you see it.

Sports fandom is a perfect example. Maybe your client lives in Dallas, but when the Packers win a big playoff game, that's when you reach out—because you remembered he grew up in Wisconsin and never shook the green-and-gold loyalty. That little touchpoint, especially in the middle of the noise around him, will stand out. It tells him you care enough to remember what really matters to him, not just the obvious details.

Marking the moments is less about grand gestures than it is about pattern recognition. People reveal what matters to them all the time— in passing comments, quick stories, throwaway lines. The discipline is listening closely, storing those details, and then reflecting them back at the right time. That's when people feel seen. That's when connection moves from professional to personal.

How to Apply

- **Notice the details.** Pay attention when people mention their family, their alma mater, their passions, or even what frustrates them. Those small details are the raw material for connection. Write them down if you have to.
- **Create a simple system.** Don't rely on memory alone. Use your calendar, a notes app, or even a spreadsheet to capture birthdays, milestones, or favorite teams. The system doesn't need to be elaborate—it just needs to be consistent.
- **Show up physically.** Texts and emails matter, but nothing substitutes for presence. Go to the funeral, attend the ribbon-cutting, buy a ticket when they're being honored. Your body in the room says more than any message you could send.
- **Celebrate in joy and stand firm in loss.** People expect you to acknowledge the big promotions or victories; they don't always expect you to show up when things go sideways. Doing both proves your connection isn't conditional.

When you put these practices side by side—*Finding the Thread, Building the Bridge*, and *Marking the Moment*—you start to see a pattern. Connection isn't about one grand gesture; it's about a series of deliberate choices. Sometimes it means slowing down to hear the story that really matters. Sometimes it means leaning on someone you already trust to help you reach the person you don't. And sometimes it means simply showing up.

So if connection is this powerful, why do so many leaders fall short? Well, it's not lack of opportunity—it's the obstacles that get in the way. In the next section, we'll look at the most common traps that break connection before it ever takes root—and how you can avoid them.

Even with the best intentions, connection doesn't always come naturally. CEOs operate under relentless pressure, and the very habits that make them effective in some areas—speed, efficiency, control—can undermine their ability to build genuine bonds. It's not external competitors that most often derail connection; it's internal defaults. Busyness, transactional thinking, or the instinct to keep people at arm's length can all get in the way. Before we close this chapter, it's worth pausing to name these obstacles clearly, because once you can see them, you can avoid them.

- **Busyness as a Badge.** CEOs often wear packed calendars like armor. The busier you are, the more important you must be. This mindset can sometimes kill connection. People feel it immediately when you're rushing, distracted, or treating them like another line item.
- **Transactional Mindset.** It's easy to slip into seeing every relationship in terms of utility: What can this person do for me? But the moment others sense they're being used, trust evaporates. True connection requires flipping the script—investing in people without a scoreboard running in the background.
- **Performative Gestures.** Sending flowers after a funeral, posting a congratulatory LinkedIn comment, firing off a quick "Happy Birthday" text—these are fine, but if they're the only moves you make, they ring hollow. People know when you're checking the box versus showing up with intent.
- **Delegating Connection.** Many leaders outsource their relationship building—asking assistants to send the notes, the gifts, the reminders. But connection can't be delegated. A handwritten note in your own words carries more weight than any polished gift basket from a chief of staff.
- **Fear of Vulnerability.** Connection means letting people see more than the polished CEO facade. Many leaders resist this out of fear it will weaken their authority. In reality, measured vulnerability strengthens connection—it humanizes you and invites reciprocity.

The good news is that every one of these obstacles has an antidote. Busyness is countered by being deliberate. Transactional habits are undone by finding the thread and treating people as more than a title. Distance shrinks when you're willing to build the bridge. And neglect disappears when you consistently mark the moments. The tools in this chapter aren't complicated—but they require vigilance. Connection is too important to leave to chance. If you want to lead with influence, you have to guard against the traps that pull you back into isolation.

Think of connection as the handshake—it opens the door. Alignment is what happens once you step inside the room and start working together. The most successful CEOs don't stop at making people feel seen; they translate that feeling into common ground and shared direction. Next, we'll explore how to build *alignment*: the discipline of ensuring that everyone—board, team, collaborators, customers—is moving with clarity toward the same horizon.

QUICK RELATIONSHIP AUDIT

Ask yourself:

- Do I take time to *find the thread*—the deeper story, value, or interest that matters to the other person?
- When I don't know someone well, do I *build the bridge* by leaning on shared contacts or genuine effort to shorten the distance?
- Do I consistently *mark the moments*—both big milestones and the small touchpoints that show I'm paying attention?
- Am I showing up in ways that feel personal and authentic, not performative or transactional?
- Have I let busyness or convenience become an excuse for neglecting connection?

KEY TAKEAWAYS

- **Connection is the foundation of relational leadership.** Without connection, nothing else in CARPE works.
- **Use tools to build connection practice.** Tools like *finding the thread*, *building the bridge*, and *marking the moments* turn connection from an accident into a discipline.
- **Connection isn't charisma.** Presence, attention, and authenticity are the things that really build trust and are the foundation of great relationships.
- **Focus on what matters.** The biggest obstacles—busyness, transactional habits, distance, neglect—are overcome with intention and consistency.
- **Seek a deep connection.** When you connect deeply, you earn trust, create clarity, and unlock energy in every relationship that matters.

Chapter 8

ALIGN

On a rainy evening in London, Tom Holland sat in a low-lit pub, a pint in front of him, the clink of glasses filling the silence he couldn't shake. He should have been in a studio, zipped into the red-and-blue suit, swinging across green screens and skylines. Instead, he was here—three pints in, restless, stuck in limbo. Spider-Man's future had been cut off not by the Green Goblin or Doctor Octopus, but by something far worse: lawyers, accountants, and studio executives.

The deal between Sony and Disney—the one that had allowed Spider-Man to swing into the Marvel Cinematic Universe—had unraveled. Disney wanted a bigger share of the profits. Sony wanted more creative control. Both wanted to win. The partnership collapsed, and with it the promise that Spider-Man would continue to fight alongside the Avengers.

For the fans, it was heartbreaking. For Holland, it was unbearable. His spidey sense told him this wasn't how the story was supposed to end. Spider-Man wasn't meant to vanish because two corporations couldn't split the spoils. Something felt off, and he knew what could bring it back into alignment: the fans.

So he did something almost no actor ever does. He picked up his phone and he called Bob Iger, the CEO of Disney. Not through his agent. Not through his manager. Holland called Iger directly himself.

Later, Iger would recall the conversation: "We spoke. And he was crying." Holland insists he wasn't crying, but admits he was emotional. He wasn't talking about box office numbers or merchandising rights. He was talking about kids. About what Spider-Man meant to them. About what it meant to the universe Marvel had built.

He said: "We built something really special. The fans deserve it."

In that moment, Holland wasn't the polished movie star. He was Peter Parker—just a kid, scared but determined to do the right thing. He wasn't fighting for fame or power. He was fighting for the people who believed in the mask.

And somehow, it worked. The studios found their way back to the table. New terms were drafted. Spider-Man stayed in the MCU and some of the biggest blockbusters in film history were created with Spider-Man at the center of the action. Not because executives grew wiser, but because an actor—barely in his twenties—reminded them of the only alignment that truly mattered: the audience.

Like in the last chapter, we'll follow a rhythm here. First, we'll look at why alignment matters in critical relationships for CEOs. Then we'll move into the practical tools you can use to create alignment with your most important relationships. Finally, we'll name the obstacles that can derail it, so you know what to watch for. The goal, as always, isn't theory. It's practice—something you can take into your next meeting, conversation, or negotiation.

WHY *ALIGNING* MATTERS

If connection is the starting line, alignment is the map. Once you've built trust, people lean in—but if they lean in different directions, you won't get very far. Alignment is what makes sure the energy of a team, a board, a shareholder, or even a vendor is harnessed toward the same horizon. Without it, progress splinters.

For most CEOs, alignment with their leadership team is the obvious place to start. And it's true—teams thrive when they share clarity on goals and priorities. But relational leadership demands more than that. A CEO has to align across the whole ecosystem: shareholders who may have different time horizons, regulators with different pressures, vendors with their own financial goals, and communities who care less about quarterly numbers and more about long-term impact.

Patrick Lencioni calls alignment "the multiplier of trust." Without it, even the best-connected leaders find themselves in gridlock. A board member thinks the company should double down on cost cutting while the CEO is investing in growth. A vendor assumes your priority is speed when what you actually need is differentiated quality. A community thinks you're retreating from local investment when, in fact, you're expanding. Each party may have valid concerns, but unless you as the leader surface them, align them, and articulate the shared purpose, energy gets wasted in conflict instead of progress.

Alignment in relationships is not a luxury. It's the CEO's job. If you don't actively work at it, you'll default to misalignment, and misalignment erodes trust just as quickly as a broken promise. The real art is getting clear on your own priorities, learning the language that creates common ground, and establishing a cadence that keeps everyone rowing in rhythm.

HOW TO PRACTICE IT: TOOLS AND TACTICS

Alignment doesn't happen by chance. It comes about through a discipline—one that requires you as the CEO to slow down, surface assumptions, and keep pulling people toward common ground. Left unchecked, even the most talented teams, boards, or partners drift. The best leaders make alignment explicit, intentional, and repeatable. They surface the goals, clarify the language, and keep a steady rhythm so that people stay in sync even as conditions change.

In practice, alignment comes down to three tools: clarity, language, and cadence. These are the tools leaders can use to transform goodwill into coordinated action. Each one is simple in concept but powerful in impact when applied consistently. This section offers three tools that make alignment practical. Each one is something you can apply whether you're running a board meeting, negotiating with an investor, or keeping your executive team moving toward the same horizon:

- **Clarity:** Surfacing and naming the goals on both sides, so no one is left guessing about what matters most.
- **Language of Alignment:** Choosing the words, metaphors, and framing that ensure people actually mean the same thing when they nod in agreement.
- **Cadence of Alignment:** Setting a rhythm of check-ins and touchpoints that keep everyone moving in sync, even as conditions change.

These tools don't require perfection, they require discipline. With them, you can shrink the gap between competing agendas, avoid the missteps that derail trust, and keep relationships focused on what really matters.

CLARITY

There was no one better at the art of clarity than Steve Jobs. When Jobs returned to Apple in 1997, the company was a mess. The product line looked like a junk drawer—dozens of computers, printers, handheld devices, each with confusing names and overlapping features. Engineers were shipping products because they could, not because they should. Customers didn't know what Apple stood for anymore. The company had brains, talent, and history, but no clarity.

Jobs did what only Jobs would do: He walked into a meeting with his senior team, grabbed a marker, and drew a simple 2×2 grid on a whiteboard. Across the top: "Consumer" and "Pro." Down the side: "Desktop" and "Laptop." Four boxes. Four products. That was it. Everything else—years of work, pet projects, sacred cows—was cut.

The room was stunned. Whole divisions disappeared overnight.

But Jobs wasn't being reckless. He was making the company clear. "Deciding what not to do is as important as deciding what to do," he said. And in those four boxes, Apple found itself again.

That discipline carried forward. When Apple launched the iPod, competitors loaded theirs with features—FM radios, expandable storage, endless buttons. Apple shipped one with a single purpose: to provide "1,000 songs in your pocket." When it came time to reinvent the phone, Jobs insisted on one button—just one. Designers pushed for more, engineers argued for complexity, but Jobs stripped the device down until it was simple enough for a child to use. His obsession wasn't aesthetics. It was clarity.

Jobs summed it up: "Simple can be harder than complex. You have to work hard to get your thinking clean to make it simple."

Jobs's discipline around clarity wasn't just about products—it's a principle that applies directly to relationships. Confusion is poison in business relationships. If people aren't sure where you stand, what you value, or what you expect, they fill in the blanks with their own assumptions. And assumptions rarely align.

As a CEO, clarity is one of the most powerful tools you have to build trust and alignment with others. Shareholders want clarity on your strategy and how you'll create value. Regulators want clarity on how you'll stay compliant. Customers want clarity on what your product delivers and why it matters. And the people on your team want clarity on what success looks like, what role they play in it, and how you'll measure progress.

Clarity in alignment isn't a one-way broadcast. It's not just about making your goals easy to understand; it's about surfacing the goals, concerns, and expectations of the other side and then ensuring both are visible.

How to Apply

- **Name your priorities simply.** Define what matters most to you in language anyone can grasp. One sentence is better than a paragraph.

- **Invite the other side's clarity.** Ask explicitly: "What's most important to you in this?" "What would success look like from your perspective?" Their answers are often the real leverage points.
- **Surface trade-offs together.** Don't just declare what you're not doing—ask what they're willing to walk away from, too. Alignment comes as much from shared sacrifices as from shared wins.
- **Check for echoes.** Summarize what you've heard from them, and ask them to do the same for you. Misalignment almost always shows up in the recap.
- **Document the core.** Whether it's a one-page memo, a short email, or a few bullet points after a meeting, put the clarified priorities in writing so everyone has the same map.

Clarity is about making sure everyone can see the same horizon line. When both sides have named their priorities, their trade-offs, and their shared goals in simple, unmistakable terms, alignment becomes possible.

LANGUAGE OF ALIGNMENT

If clarity is about knowing *what* matters, language is about knowing *how* to say it so people align around it. The two are different disciplines. You can be clear in your own mind yet fail to bring others with you. Alignment happens when clarity is translated into words that resonate—words that inspire, simplify, and stick.

That's why we're staying with Steve Jobs. He was not only the master of clarity; he was the master of language. Jobs understood that language is the bridge between a leader's vision and a team's commitment. It's how strategy becomes a story.

Think of the iPod. Jobs could have described it as a "5GB MP3 player with FireWire support." That would have been technically clear, but not aligning. Instead, he said: "1,000 songs in your pocket." One phrase, and suddenly customers, employees, and investors were aligned around the same picture. The engineers weren't just building a device; they were putting a thousand songs in your pocket.

Or take the "Think Different" campaign. At the time, Apple was struggling to regain relevance against Microsoft. Internally, Jobs needed to rally employees; externally, he needed to reconnect with customers. "Think Different" was more than marketing—it was a declaration. It told employees who they were, told customers why Apple existed, and told shareholders what Apple stood for. Clarity of purpose became language of alignment.

Jobs put it simply: "The most powerful person in the world is the storyteller. The storyteller sets the vision, values, and agenda for an entire generation that is to come."

Mastering language isn't just about dazzling audiences at a product launch or inspiring millions through a commercial. The same principle applies in one-on-one relationships. The words you choose in a boardroom negotiation, a feedback session with a direct report, or a call with a key supplier can either create friction or alignment. Clear, simple, resonant language is how you cut through defensiveness, clarify intent, and keep people rowing in the same direction. It's not about slogans—it's about speaking in a way that makes the other person feel included in the story.

How to Apply

- **Choose simplicity over jargon.** Drop the buzzwords and acronyms. Use plain language that people can repeat easily to others.
- **Frame around "we," not "I."** Words that emphasize shared goals ("we need to get this done together") signal partnership, while "I" and "you" can unintentionally create opposition.
- **Name the shared horizon.** Whether it's "protecting the community," "building a legacy," or "serving our customers," put the bigger goal into words that everyone can point to.
- **Repeat with consistency.** Alignment language only works if it's consistent. A phrase or framing repeated across conversations and settings becomes an anchor point everyone remembers.

If clarity sets the direction and language creates understanding, cadence keeps everyone moving in rhythm. Alignment isn't a one-time event; it must be reinforced over and over. Verne Harnish has repeatedly said, "Routine sets you free," and he's right. Without a rhythm, even the best intentions scatter.

CADENCE OF ALIGNMENT

For me, cadence has been one of the most powerful tools in building businesses and relationships across all six relationship arenas. The key relationships that mattered most—my board, my senior leadership team, my customers, my vendors, my lawyers, my community—didn't stay aligned by accident. They stayed aligned because I made time for them, regularly and predictably.

That meant annual strategic retreats with leadership teams where we reset the vision and priorities. Regular vendor reviews where we checked not just performance metrics but the health of the relationship. Routine client meetings to hear directly what mattered most to them. Even regulators and community partners became part of this rhythm, through standing check-ins, lunches, or roundtables. By putting these meetings on the calendar—yearly, quarterly, monthly, weekly—I was signaling that alignment was not an afterthought but a responsibility.

The rhythm of alignment isn't about endless meetings. It's about creating touchpoints that prevent drift. Just like a coach holds weekly practices and film sessions to keep the team on the same page, a CEO must design a cadence that ensures relationships across all arenas don't fall out of sync.

How to Apply

- **Set the rhythm.** Decide what touchpoints belong on your calendar: annual retreats, quarterly reviews, monthly check-ins, weekly one-on-ones.

- **Make it predictable.** Cadence creates trust. People align more easily when they know the next conversation is already scheduled.
- **Tailor the rhythm by arena.** Not every relationship needs the same tempo—clients may require quarterly reviews, vendors semi-annual, your team weekly.
- **Protect the time.** Don't let urgent tasks cannibalize the rhythm. When cadence slips, alignment fractures.
- **Use meetings as alignment, not updates.** The purpose is not reporting—it's ensuring goals, expectations, and perspectives stay connected.

Clear goals, shared language, and a steady rhythm make alignment possible—but they don't make it permanent. Missteps still happen, and often in predictable ways. Before we close this chapter, let's look at the traps that undo alignment and how to avoid them.

COMMON OBSTACLES AND HOW TO AVOID THEM

These are the patterns I see most often when CEOs lose alignment. They aren't dramatic failures, but small, familiar slips that quietly erode trust and clarity:

- **One-Sided Clarity.** CEOs often get crystal clear on *their own* goals but forget to check in on the other side of the table. A vendor's priorities may shift, a shareholder's time horizon may shorten, or a team member's personal situation may change. If you never stop to ask, "Has anything changed for you?" you risk working off an outdated map.
- **The Fog of Complexity.** Leaders love detail—but sometimes too much detail becomes the enemy. Agreements buried in forty-slide decks or sixty-page memos blur what really matters. When expectations aren't boiled down to a few simple lines, people walk away with different interpretations of the same conversation.
- **Assumed Alignment.** Silence doesn't equal agreement. Just

because no one raised objections in the boardroom doesn't mean everyone is aligned. Teams (and stakeholders) often nod along but walk out with conflicting interpretations. If alignment isn't explicitly confirmed, you can be sure it's only partial.

- **Misaligned Cadence.** Even when people agree on direction, alignment drifts over time. A board that meets quarterly may lose touch with what's happening weekly. A leadership team that only talks strategy once a year will find execution veering off course. Without regular checkpoints, small misalignments compound into major gaps.

Alignment isn't lost in big explosions—it slips away through small cracks: assumptions that go unchecked, complexity that fogs the signal, silence mistaken for agreement, meetings that come too late, or egos that crowd out shared purpose. The antidote is the very discipline we've outlined in this chapter: *clarity* to strip the noise down to what truly matters, *language* to ensure everyone hears the same message the same way, and *cadence* to check in before misalignment drifts too far. Keep these habits alive, and alignment becomes a practiced rhythm that holds every relationship steady.

Alignment is powerful, but it's not permanent. Even when you achieve it, the world doesn't stop moving—markets shift, competitors emerge, people change their minds. That's where the next discipline comes in: *respond*. If alignment is about creating a shared direction, responding is about what you do when reality doesn't follow the script. The best CEOs aren't just clear and consistent; they're adaptive. In the next chapter, we'll look at how leaders respond in real time—turning setbacks into signals, staying calm under fire, and showing their people how to move forward when the unexpected happens.

Ask yourself:

- Do I make my goals and priorities unmistakably clear—and do I take time to understand the goals and priorities of the other side?
- Am I using simple, shared language that reduces misinterpretation rather than increasing it?
- Do I write things down in plain terms so expectations are visible, not just implied?
- Have I established a cadence—regular check-ins, meetings, or reviews—that keeps alignment from drifting over time?
- When disagreements surface, do I push for clarity and common ground, or do I let misalignment linger beneath the surface?

KEY TAKEAWAYS

- **Alignment is the glue that holds relationships together.** Without alignment, even the best intentions collapse into missteps and mistrust.
- **Clarity is step one.** Make your priorities known, and take the time to understand the other side's priorities too.
- **Language of alignment matters.** Choose words that are simple, shared, and resonant so everyone is speaking the same language.
- **Cadence keeps alignment from drifting.** Regular check-ins, meetings, and reviews create rhythm and prevent surprises.
- **Misalignment rarely comes from bad actors.** It comes from neglect, complexity, or assuming everyone sees the world the same way.
- **CEOs are responsible for alignment with all stakeholders.** CEOs don't just manage alignment inside their teams—they're responsible for alignment with boards, shareholders, vendors, customers, and communities.

Chapter 9

RESPOND

October 1962. The Cabinet Room of the White House was thick with cigarette smoke and tension. Intelligence photos had just confirmed what many feared: Soviet nuclear missiles were being installed in Cuba, ninety miles from Florida. Each missile could obliterate an American city in minutes.

Around the table, generals and advisors pounded their case. "We need to strike," one insisted. "Air strikes. Invasion. Take them out before they're operational." The military argued that anything less would look weak. Others, more cautious, warned that striking Cuba could unleash a chain reaction leading straight to nuclear war.

In the middle sat President John F. Kennedy, his face calm but his mind racing. Every option before him was catastrophic. If he acted rashly, millions could die. If he hesitated, the Soviets might see weakness and press further. The weight of the Cold War pressed down on his shoulders.

Behind closed doors, John leaned on his younger brother Robert. Together, they looked for another path. They knew they had to act— but not just act. They had to respond.

That's when the letters arrived.

Within twenty-four hours, two very different messages came from Soviet Premier Nikita Khrushchev.

The first was long, rambling, even emotional. It hinted at a way out: If the United States pledged not to invade Cuba, the Soviets would dismantle the missiles. It was raw, almost desperate, but it left an opening.

The second was the opposite. Stern. Demanding. It insisted the US also remove its Jupiter missiles from Turkey—a deal that would be politically toxic in Washington. To many of Kennedy's advisors, this hardline letter represented the "real" Soviet position. They urged him to respond in kind, to meet force with force.

Two letters. Two voices. Which one would they answer?

The Kennedys understood something critical: Khrushchev was under pressure, too—trapped between hawks and pragmatists in Moscow. If the US focused on the hard-line message, they'd box him in. The confrontation would spiral. But if they answered the first letter—the softer one—they would give him room to step back without losing face.

So they made their move. They ignored the bluster and answered only the conciliatory note. They sent a carefully worded reply, offering public assurances not to invade Cuba, while quietly signaling willingness to discuss Turkey later through back channels.

It was a gamble. But it worked. Days later, Soviet ships turned back. The missiles were dismantled. The world exhaled.

The Cuban Missile Crisis didn't end with missiles fired. It ended with words chosen.

That's the essence of *respond* in the CARPE framework. Anyone can react—slam the table, issue threats, act on impulse. But great leaders pause. They weigh not only the facts in front of them, but also how the other side will interpret their move. They recognize the human need for dignity, even in conflict.

The Kennedys didn't "win" the crisis by overpowering the Soviets. They resolved it by responding with poise and precision, in a way that preserved dignity on both sides—and pulled the world back from the brink.

In CARPE, respond reminds us that leadership is not about avoiding hard choices. It's about choosing how to act so that the relationship survives the moment. Respond means you can disagree without disrespect, correct without humiliating, and lead without alienating.

WHY *RESPONDING* MATTERS

Respond is the discipline of thoughtful action. It's not waiting forever, and it's not firing off the first instinct that comes to mind. Respond means being considerate of the relationship, strategic about the stakes, and still taking action when it counts.

As a CEO, you don't have the luxury of sitting on the sidelines. People look to you in moments of uncertainty, conflict, or crisis. If you freeze, they lose confidence. If you overreact, they lose trust. But when you respond—thoughtfully, deliberately, and decisively—you model the kind of leadership that strengthens relationships instead of fraying them.

This matters across every arena of leadership. Shareholders want to see that you can respond to shifting markets without panicking. Employees want to see you handle setbacks with calm, not anger. Vendors want a partner who will respond when problems arise, not vanish into silence. Communities want to see that you respond to their concerns, not just their applause.

Respond is not passive. It's the opposite. It is action with intention. It's the ability to slow down just long enough to see the full picture, and then to act in a way that preserves trust, protects dignity, and moves things forward.

When you look back at the Cuban Missile Crisis, what made the Kennedys effective wasn't that they simply stayed calm. It was that they *chose* how to act. They considered options, weighed perceptions, and then crafted a response that lowered the temperature instead of raising it. That's what leaders do: They pause long enough to see what the moment really requires—and then they move.

As a CEO, people won't remember whether you were the first

to react; they'll remember whether you responded in a way that moved things forward. A strong response balances speed with intention: quick enough to matter, thoughtful enough to last. That kind of response requires structure, not guesswork. The next section outlines the tools you can use to build that structure into your leadership.

HOW TO PRACTICE IT: TOOLS AND TACTICS

Responding well is about deliberate action. It is not about "going with your gut" as some will cavalierly tell you. People are waiting, watching, and drawing conclusions from how you move. The goal isn't to act first or fastest—it's to act in a way that reinforces trust, strengthens relationships, and moves things forward. That takes tools you can use under pressure.

In practice, there are three tools you can use to turn intention into action:

- **Get the Right Information:** Ensure you're acting on facts, not assumptions, by creating a system to keep you properly informed.
- **Pause, Then Decide:** Insert a deliberate beat before acting, long enough to weigh the impact on relationships as well as outcomes and enough time for you to properly respond.
- **Close the Loop:** Finish the cycle by circling back so people know not only what you decided, but why you made the decision.

These three tools create a rhythm in how your actions build great, long-term relationships as a CEO. You start by grounding yourself in reality, taking the necessary pause to choose wisely, and then making sure the people around you feel informed and included in the response. That's how a moment of crisis or uncertainty becomes an opportunity to strengthen alignment and trust.

The deal looked perfect on paper. Nine acres in one of the fastest growing municipalities in the county—exactly where the population was shifting, where new rental housing was needed most. My client Chuck, a seasoned developer, ran the numbers: zoning change, market demand, projected returns. Everything pointed to success.

He bid aggressively and won. The city commission seemed favorable to the rezoning, and the project was set to move forward. But there was one person he hadn't truly understood—the mayor. The mayor wasn't thinking about long-term housing needs or future voters. He was thinking about the people who lived there now: the ones who wanted a grocery store, a Chipotle, and a few new places to shop and eat.

The mayor wasn't opposed to change. He just wanted a *different* kind of change. Retail, not residential. And when Chuck went to pitch his plan for rental apartments—armed with data and demand projections—the mayor smiled politely and said no. The zoning didn't move. The project stalled. Chuck eventually had to bring in a new partner who specialized in retail and had the right relationships to make it work.

The lesson was painful but simple: He had the wrong information. Not inaccurate data, just incomplete understanding. He knew the *market,* but not the *mindset* of the key decision-maker.

As a CEO, this happens more often than we'd like to admit. The most dangerous mistakes don't come from bad math, but from our blind spots. Your job isn't just to collect facts, but to make sure you're seeing the whole field, including the human factors.

Daniel Kahneman, the Nobel Prize–winning psychologist and author of *Thinking, Fast and Slow,* called this trap WYSIATI—"What You See Is All There Is." He observed that we tend to make confident judgments based only on what's visible or available, ignoring what might be missing. We fall prey to what he called the illusion of validity—believing our conclusions are sound simply because the pieces we do have fit neatly together. Even experts, Kahneman warned, are not immune. The real danger for leaders isn't bad data—it's acting on partial data while assuming it's complete.

That's where relationships come in. L. David Marquet, a former US Navy submarine captain turned leadership thinker, described the "gap between authority and information." The people with the most power rarely have the best facts. "Move the authority to where the information lives," he advised—and when you can't, you need to bring the information closer to the authority.

That means building an inner circle of truth tellers. These are people who aren't afraid to say, "You're missing something." It means identifying who in your network actually has their ear to the ground, who can read the room when you can't.

Good information requires nuance. It's knowing when a board member's support is wavering, when a team member's focus has shifted, when a long-time client's trust is fraying. You can't pull that from a spreadsheet. You get it through relationships, through the people who see and hear what you can't.

How to Apply

- **Map your sources of truth.** Identify the handful of people inside and outside your organization who give you clear, reliable insight. Keep that list short—and keep it close.
- **Ask for the story behind the numbers.** Every metric has a human context. Ask what's driving the trend, not just what the trend is.
- **Check your blind spots.** Ask yourself, *What don't I know? What might I be missing?* Make it a habit.
- **Diversify your inputs.** Don't rely on one channel for critical insight—combine data, field experience, and trusted relationships.
- **Reward honesty, not accuracy.** When people know they can tell you hard truths without penalty, you'll get better information.

Once you have the right information, the next step is resisting the instinct to move too fast. CEOs are built for action, but great leadership depends on timing as much as decision. A short pause—used wisely—builds clarity, earns trust, and shows others that you've considered the weight of the moment before acting. That's where the next tool comes in: Pause, then decide.

PAUSE, THEN DECIDE

Daniel Kahneman, whom we mentioned before, famously described two modes of thinking: System 1—fast, intuitive, emotional—and System 2—slow, deliberate, rational. Most leaders spend their days in System 1, making hundreds of quick judgments that keep the machine running. But in moments that matter—when a relationship hangs in the balance, when the stakes are high—System 2 must take the wheel. The best CEOs know when to slow the pace just enough to shift gears.

The Stoics understood this centuries earlier. You can't control what happens, only how you respond. The pause between stimulus and response is where leadership lives. That pause isn't about hesitation; it's about intention. It's where emotion meets reason, where reflex gives way to reflection. This is where you earn your credibility.

I learned this the hard way. Early in my time as a board chair—first at Apollo Bank and later at the Inter-American Foundation—I thought leadership meant being the first to answer every question. I'd respond to every comment, try to steer every conversation, swing at every pitch. My intentions were good, but I was crowding out better voices. Over time, I learned that a well-timed pause could do more than any quick reply. Sometimes another board member had a sharper insight. Sometimes the silence itself drew out a perspective I would have missed. And sometimes, the question simply didn't need an answer right then.

"Pause, then decide" doesn't mean slowing everything down. It means creating just enough space between input and action to ensure your response strengthens relationships rather than strains them. The pause gives you time to check your instincts, consider the human side of the decision, and align your response with the long game and not just the moment.

- **Insert a beat.** Even a few seconds of silence before answering prevents reactivity.
- **Separate emotion from action.** If a situation triggers frustration or urgency, don't decide at that moment. Step away—literally, if needed. Respond once your emotional temperature drops, not while it's rising.
- **Time-box the pause.** In fast-moving situations, set a short deadline so you don't slip into paralysis.

Once you've paused, weighed the facts, and made your move, your work isn't done. The strength of a response isn't just in the decision itself, but in how you close it. People watch not only *what* you decide, but *how* you follow through. Failing to circle back leaves confusion in your wake; closing the loop reinforces confidence and clarity. The final tool is about making sure your actions don't drift into ambiguity or rumor—it's about follow-through that builds trust and alignment.

CLOSE THE LOOP

You make a decision. You shift direction. You act. But how often do you make sure that everyone who matters knows *why*? In leadership, leaving a decision unannounced or unexplained is like dropping a stone in a pond and walking away without watching the ripples. The question isn't just, *Did you respond?* It's, *Did your response land?*

Robert Cialdini, the psychologist who wrote *Influence*, offers a simple truth about why closing the loop matters so much. One of his core principles is Consistency and Commitment—once people have agreed to something, even informally, they feel a natural pull to stay consistent with that commitment. It's how trust and predictability are built.

So, when you make a change—a new direction, a shift in priorities, an adjustment to an agreement—and don't explain it, people are left wondering, *Wait, did something change? Are we still on the same page?* That uncertainty is worse than disagreement. Cialdini found that when people sense inconsistency from their leaders, they start guessing at motives or worrying something's being hidden. It's not malice; it's human nature. We all crave coherence between what was said, what was done, and what happens next.

Consider a scenario: You renegotiate terms with a vendor behind closed doors. You believe it's the right move. But your operations team doesn't know. The customer support team doesn't know. Sales continues working under outdated assumptions. The result? Friction, duplicate efforts, blame, confusion. Even though your action was deliberate, the lack of closure causes far more waste than the concession itself.

Closing the loop should not be seen as optional, but as a way to create relational currency. It says: *I see you. I value your alignment. I'm not leaving you guessing.*

How to Apply

- **Circle back fast.** Once a decision is made, make it a habit to close the loop within twenty-four hours with anyone affected.
- **Keep it short.** A quick "Here's what we decided and why" beats a long, defensive memo.
- **Acknowledge input.** If someone's perspective shaped your decision, say so. It reinforces that their voice matters.
- **Check reactions.** Don't assume understanding—ask, "Does this make sense from your end?" It opens the door for clarity before confusion grows.
- **Model it publicly.** When your team sees you close the loop consistently, they'll start doing it too.

Even with the best intentions, these three tools—getting the right information, pausing before deciding, and closing the loop—can still break down in practice. Pressure, pace, and ego all conspire against good judgment. A CEO might skip a pause because the clock is ticking, or act on bad information because it came from a trusted voice. Sometimes you close the loop too late—or not at all—and realize only afterward how quickly trust can fray. The next section names the most common traps that can derail even experienced leaders, and how to steer clear of them.

COMMON OBSTACLES AND HOW TO AVOID THEM

Even thoughtful leaders can stumble in how they respond. The problem isn't usually lack of intelligence or intent—it's pressure. Decisions pile up, emotions run high, and speed feels like success. But when response becomes reflex instead of reflection, trust begins to crack. These are the most common traps that pull CEOs off course, and how to avoid them.

- **Acting on bad information.** Being uninformed and being misinformed are equally risky. When leaders mistake confidence for accuracy, or rely on a small circle of voices, they end up solving the wrong problem. To avoid this, build a diverse network of truth tellers and check your sources, especially the ones who always agree with you.
- **Mistaking reaction for response.** Speed feels powerful, but it's not the same as leadership. A fast reaction might satisfy the moment, but a true response shapes the outcome. Take a beat to ask, *What am I really solving for?* That pause can be the difference between damage control and direction.
- **Overcorrecting in public.** Some CEOs think decisiveness means being loud or visible, but overexposure can backfire. Respond in proportion to the moment. Not every issue needs a memo or press release; sometimes a quiet call or one-on-one conversation carries more weight.
- **Failing to close the loop.** A brilliant decision that no one understands is a wasted one. If your people are left wondering why you acted—or whether their input mattered—you've created confusion,

not clarity. Always explain your reasoning to those affected, even briefly. It turns a decision into a shared moment of alignment.

- **Letting emotion set the tone.** Responding doesn't mean suppressing emotion, but it does mean steering it. Anger, fear, or pride can leak into your message and distort the signal. Channel emotion into energy—acknowledge it privately, then act publicly from a place of intention.

Responding well is about thoughtful action—seeing clearly, acting deliberately, and closing the loop so people know where things stand. But once you've built the habit of responding, a new challenge emerges: Not every situation deserves your response, and not every relationship or issue carries equal weight. The real test of leadership is knowing where to focus your limited time and energy. That's where the next chapter—*Prioritize*—comes in. We'll look at how great leaders decide what (and who) truly matters, and how they organize their attention so the most important relationships never fall to the bottom of the list.

QUICK RELATIONSHIP AUDIT

Ask yourself:

- Do I have a reliable system for gathering both hard data and soft insight before responding?
- Have I paused long enough to interpret what's really happening— not just what's being said?
- When I do act, is my response deliberate, proportional, and rooted in the long-term relationship, not the short-term reaction?
- Do the people affected by my decisions understand why I made them?
- After a major decision or response, have I followed up to see how it landed and what impact it had?

KEY TAKEAWAYS

- **Responding is not reacting.** A great response is fast enough to matter and thoughtful enough to last.
- **Get the right information first.** Bad data or biased feedback leads to bad responses. Build a network of truth tellers who will tell you what you *need* to hear, not what you *want* to hear.
- **Pause, then decide.** A moment of reflection separates leaders who lead from those who simply react.
- **Close the loop.** Your response doesn't end with your action—it ends when everyone understands what you did, why you did it, and what happens next.
- **Intentional action builds trust.** Responding well signals stability, confidence, and care—qualities people remember long after the crisis has passed.

<u>Chapter 10</u>

PRIORITIZE

Rick Rubin, the brilliant, long-bearded, and barefoot record producer, has collaborated with more than a hundred artists across wildly different genres—Johnny Cash, Adele, the Red Hot Chili Peppers, Slayer, Tom Petty, and Public Enemy. In that breadth lies a paradox. For every album he produces, there are dozens he declines. Projects that don't align, relationships that don't resonate—artists searching for something outside the creative space Rubin occupies in that moment—never make it halfway to his studio.

When Cash agreed to record *American Recordings* with Rubin, many in the industry were surprised that he would prioritize it over so many other opportunities. By then, Cash was no longer the chart king—his relevance in popular country music had waned, and labels had long since dropped him. But Rubin had a vision that he felt could make this project truly special. Rubin proposed something risky: recording in sparse settings—often with Cash alone and acoustic—focusing on emotional truth over commercial polish. That decision changed the narrative. *American Recordings* became not just a revival, but a reinvention—one deeply rooted in the relational trust Rubin built with Cash.

This selectivity wasn't happenstance. Rubin once said, "I know what I like and what I don't like. And I'm decisive about what I like and what I don't like." That decisiveness is relational by nature—it's a boundary, a filter for preserving presence. He has also warned that "distractions can get in the way of a direct connection to the creative force." When applied to leadership, that insight becomes stark: Every ask is a distraction; every yes is a choice to withdraw energy from something else.

In *The Creative Act*, Rubin writes, "Look for what you notice but no one else sees." He suggests that the subtle signals often point to what matters most. That's why he resists spreading himself thin—he listens not to the loudest demand, but to the most meaningful one. He cautions against "demo-itis"—staying in half-formed versions too long—a metaphor for relationships that linger beyond their season.

Rubin doesn't treat every artist equally. Some collaborations are slow and deep—marked by listening, revision, retreat, and return. Others never begin—Rubin's taste, his relational calibration, refuses access when alignment is absent. Over time, his discography shows seasons of sustained partnership—Cash, Chili Peppers—and pauses where he waits, calibrates, does nothing but listen.

In leadership as in creation, clarity doesn't come from doing more—it comes from editing and prioritizing. The richest yes is validated by every no you choose.

As a CEO, you may not see your work reflected in Rubin's artistic world, but his approach offers a metaphor for relational leadership. Rubin doesn't commit to every voice, or settle for superficial participation. He invests where his presence can deepen trust and create outcomes that are worth pursuing. As a leader, your task isn't to connect wildly; it's to go deep where connection matters most.

WHY PRIORITIZING MATTERS

If there's one thing a CEO has to really learn how to control, it's their time and focus. These are truly the only things you even have the ability to control in the workplace. Everything else—markets, competitors, interest rates, talent—can shift overnight. But how you spend your hours and where you direct your attention send a powerful signal to the organization. Your focus becomes everyone's focus. When the CEO leans in, others follow.

Your time and focus, as mentioned previously in this book, are the scarcest and most valuable resources in your company. Which relationships you invest your time in communicate what matters most, whether you say it aloud or not. A CEO's calendar is the most visible form of strategy.

That's why prioritization is more than a management exercise; it's an act of leadership. If your company's growth strategy depends on acquisitions, your time should reflect that. Are you building relationships with potential targets? Are you deepening trust with your investment bankers and deal team? Or, if your strategy is centered on organic growth, are you investing in clients that align with your long-term focus—and spending meaningful time with the sales and service teams who make that growth real? Even initiatives that seem operational—like building a new headquarters—require relational strategy. Have you developed the community connections and good-will necessary to make the project possible?

At its core, prioritization is about honesty: Where do you add the most value? Some CEOs are natural dealmakers; others excel at culture, or relationships with employees, or understanding the customer. You don't need to be everywhere, but you do need to be intentional about where you show up. That's the difference between activity and impact.

Next, we'll explore how to practice that clarity—starting with the framework for sorting and managing your most important relationships.

Prioritization is the discipline of getting specific. It's about being narrow and specific—of drawing boundaries around your time and choosing where your presence can make the greatest impact. As a CEO, your job isn't to be everywhere; it's to be effective where and when it counts.

Every week brings more requests than you can possibly meet: clients who want attention, board members who want updates, community leaders who want your voice, employees who want your ear. You can't say yes to them all—and you shouldn't. Prioritization is the process of ranking what matters most, not only for the company's goals but for the unique value that you bring as its leader. Some relationships will always be important to the business, but that doesn't mean you're the one who should nurture them. The most effective CEOs know when their direct involvement adds value—and when their time is better spent elsewhere.

To help you practice that kind of precision, the next three tools turn the concept of prioritization into something visible, measurable, and repeatable:

- **High Payoff Activities (HPAs):** Identify the interactions and efforts where you create the most value for the organization—and align them with your unique strengths.
- **Relationship Zones:** Sort your relationships by strategic relevance and energy, so you know where to double down, where to delegate, and where to let go.
- **The Relationship Prioritization Map:** A visual audit that reveals where your time and attention are actually going—and where they should go next.

These tools will help you see prioritization not as restrictions but as liberation. When you know who and what deserves your focus, every no becomes an investment in the right yes. Let's begin with the first: high payoff activities.

HIGH PAYOFF ACTIVITIES

Peter Drucker once said, "There is nothing so useless as doing efficiently that which should not be done at all." It's a reminder that not all activity is progress—and not all engagement is value. For a CEO, the most precious and finite resource isn't money; it's focused attention.

High Payoff Activities are the small handful of actions and interactions that generate an outsized return for the business and the relationships that sustain it. These are the moments where your presence, perspective, or decision truly changes the outcome.

Every leader has their version. For some, it's meeting with a handful of your company's top customers who drive your most profitable growth. For others, it's mentoring the two or three executives who will determine whether the next growth phase succeeds. It might be spending an hour each week with your head of sales, refining how the company shows up in the market. It's the difference between being busy and being effective.

What I see over and over is CEOs who confuse preference for payoff. They do what they like doing—drafting the presentation, playing golf with the same clients every weekend, sitting in on a marketing brainstorm—because it feels productive or familiar. But the question isn't what you enjoy; it's what creates disproportionate value. High Payoff Activities are those few relational moves that ripple through the organization, shaping trust, alignment, and performance far beyond your direct reach.

To identify them, you have to know where you personally add the most value. Some CEOs are visionaries—they need to be in the rooms where big ideas are shaped. Others are operators—they add value when they're coaching, refining, or asking hard questions. Some thrive in building external relationships—with investors, regulators, or strategic partners—while others do their best work deep inside the culture. The point isn't to mimic another CEO's rhythm. It's to design your own.

Over time, your HPAs should align with your company's priorities. If you're pursuing M&A, your high-payoff zone might be time spent cultivating relationships with acquisition targets or investment bankers. If the priority is customer retention, your payoff may come from direct client engagement or supporting the frontline team. If you're rolling out a new product line, it might mean investing in relationships with your distribution channel partners and field sales people in order to generate excitement and get new ideas.

High Payoff Activities are rarely urgent. They don't shout for your attention. But they compound. Every week you spend time in your HPA zone, you're shaping the long-term trajectory of the business.

How to Apply

- **Define your area of impact.** Ask yourself: "Where does my presence create the biggest ripple effect?" If it's unclear, track where major wins or breakthroughs tend to originate—and where your input consistently moves things forward.
- **Audit your calendar.** Look back over the last month. What percentage of your time was spent on high-payoff interactions versus maintenance tasks or ceremonial meetings? The number rarely lies.
- **Protect your time.** Block recurring windows for your HPAs. Don't let urgency hijack them. A single uninterrupted hour in your highest-leverage work is worth more than a full day scattered across noise.
- **Align with strategy.** Revisit your company's top three objectives and ask which relationships directly tie into them. That's where your HPA focus should go.
- **Delegate the rest.** If it doesn't require your unique value, empower someone else. Freeing yourself from the low payoff allows others to grow—and keeps you focused where you matter most.

Once you've defined where your time has the greatest impact, the next step is clarity about who deserves that time. Responsible relational leadership relies on managing access. Being honest about what you're good at, where your presence drives performance, and where it doesn't, helps you redirect attention toward the relationships that move the company forward. The question now shifts from what you do to who you do it with—and that's where the Relationship Zones come in.

THE RELATIONSHIP ZONES

It took me five years to realize I was giving my best hours to the wrong person. We'll call him Steve.

Steve was one of the first people to support Apollo Bank back when the idea felt impossible. This was during the middle of the great financial crisis, when legacy financial institutions were collapsing and I was working to start a brand-new bank. Steve believed in me. He opened one of our first accounts, made introductions, and was a vocal supporter when few others were. In those early months, when I was running on fumes, Steve's belief gave me confidence.

So I gave him access. I took every request for a meeting, took all his calls on the first ring, and gave him the kind of attention reserved for my top clients. But as the years went by, the dynamic changed. His business didn't grow with ours. His requests got bigger, but his impact got smaller. He wanted special treatment, exceptions, personal attention—without contributing meaningfully to the company's growth.

Meanwhile, other, more valuable relationships weren't getting my time. My leadership team noticed and it was impacting our culture. One day, one of my executives said it out loud: "You know you meet with Steve more than our top three clients combined?"

That's when it hit me: I wasn't being loyal. I was being avoidant. I was maintaining a relationship out of habit—and guilt—long after it stopped serving the mission.

When I finally redefined the relationship, everything changed. Instead of monthly meetings, we met once a year for dinner. It was meaningful but proportionate. I thanked him for his early support, stayed connected, but moved him to the right place in my mental map. It wasn't a demotion—it was the right thing to do for him, me, and our company.

That clarity forced me to ask: Where else was I spending time out of history instead of impact?

Not every relationship deserves equal access or equal time. Some are essential to your company's direction and culture; others matter situationally. Many, like Steve, once played a vital role but now belong to a different phase of your business.

As a CEO, your time and attention are leadership capital. They communicate value more powerfully than any memo or speech. If your calendar isn't aligned with your strategy, neither is your organization.

Before you can prioritize, you have to sort. That's what the Relationship Zones framework helps you do—get clear about who truly needs your focus, and who can thrive with less of it.

THE RELATIONSHIP ZONES

Core Relationships

Mission-critical connections that shape direction and culture

Strategic Relationships

Important at specific moments, maintained for engagement when needed

Legacy Relationships

Once important but no longer in alignment, requiring respect and boundaries

The Three Relationship Zones:

- **Core Relationships:** These are your mission-critical connections that align with the most important goals of your company. They shape the company's direction and culture. These deserve your best energy, consistent time, and direct access.
- **Strategic Relationships:** These are important, but they matter

most during specific moments—product launches, acquisitions, expansions, or crises. They need you to be present when it counts, not every week. Keep them warm, consistent, and ready for engagement when the time comes.

- **Legacy or Draining Relationships:** These are relationships that once mattered deeply but no longer align with where you're going. They may still carry emotion, history, or influence—but your regular interaction with them doesn't move the company forward. These require respect and boundaries. Reframe them rather than sever them.

Knowing who belongs in which zone allows you to direct your time like you would any other scarce resource.

How to Apply

- **List your relationships.** List the twenty people or relationships who consume most of your time. Add the ones who should be on that list—those most vital to the company's current and future success. Include relationships from across all the relationship arenas outlined earlier in this book.
- **Identify the gaps.** Once you've built your list, step back and ask: Who's missing? Are there high-value relationships you're neglecting because they're not loud, convenient, or familiar? Are there people whose input could unlock growth, reduce risk, or open doors, but you've been "too busy" to reach out?
- **Sort by zone.** Place each relationship into one of the three zones—Core, Strategic, or Legacy. Be candid about where they belong today, not where they once fit. This is about the present and the future, not nostalgia.
- **Match cadence to zone.** Adjust your calendar accordingly. Core relationships deserve predictable access; Strategic ones get focused attention during key windows; legacy ones move to respectful but limited touchpoints.

Once you've sorted your relationships into zones, patterns start to emerge. You'll see where your energy is compounding—and where it's leaking. But awareness isn't enough. To act with intention, you need a way to visualize those trade-offs, to see on one page where your time and attention truly go versus where they should go. That's where the Relationship Prioritization Map comes in. It turns insight into action.

THE RELATIONSHIP PRIORITIZATION MAP

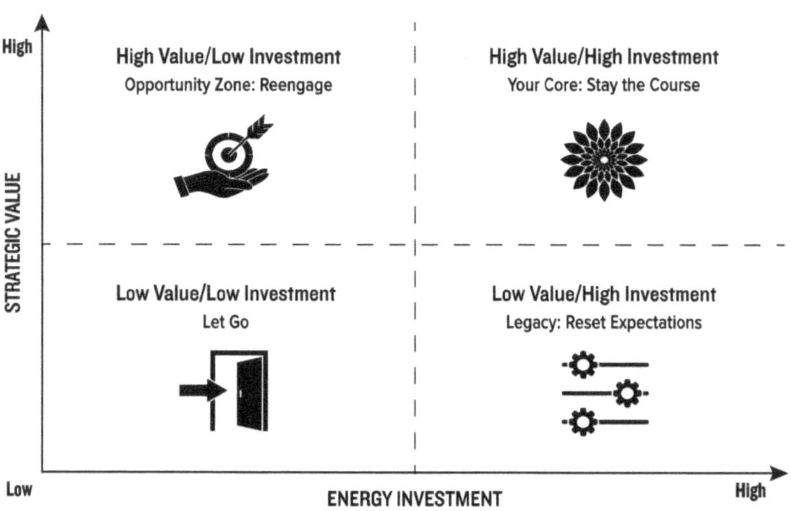

Once you've sorted your relationships into zones, the next step is to see them—literally. The Relationship Prioritization Map is a simple but revealing tool that turns reflection into data. It shows you where your energy is compounding and where it's being drained. It forces you to translate instinct into insight: Who am I spending time with? And does that reflect who matters most to our future? Think of it as a visual snapshot of how your leadership attention is distributed.

The vertical axis measures Strategic Value—how critical a relationship is to your company's success and long-term goals. The horizontal axis measures Investment—how much time, expense, presence, and emotional bandwidth you're giving that person or entity. Once you plot your key relationships across those two axes, the truth becomes hard to ignore. You'll see where you're overinvested, underinvested, or perfectly aligned.

The exercise reveals whether your calendar and your company's priorities are telling the same story. In my experience, most CEOs are surprised by what they find.

How to Use the Map

Start by writing down the names of the fifteen to twenty people or entities who currently occupy the most space in your week: board members, clients, senior leaders, vendors, advisors, and even legacy relationships that still command your time. Then add the ones who should be on that list—the partners, prospects, or future collaborators essential to your company's next chapter. Don't limit yourself to who's loudest or most familiar; include the quiet but strategic relationships that might be going undernourished.

Once you have the list, plot each name on a two-by-two grid.

- **The vertical axis:** Strategic Value (low → high) Measures how vital this relationship is to your company's long-term goals, growth, or stability.
- **The horizontal axis:** Energy Investment (low → high) Reflects how much time, attention, and emotional energy you currently give this person or group.

You'll end up with four quadrants:

1. **High Value/High Investment: Stay the course.** These are your core relationships. Double down.

2. **High Value/Low Investment: Reengage.** This is the opportunity zone. You're underinvested in relationships that could transform your business.
3. **Low Value/High Investment: Reset expectations.** These are legacy or draining relationships. This is a danger zone and you need to really make a decision if you need to delegate, redefine, or reduce time spent.
4. **Low Value/Low Investment: Let go.** You don't need to maintain every relationship, and you need to get comfortable with the fact that the by-product of prioritization is that something will simply get no attention or need closure.

The point isn't to reduce people to coordinates—it's to see how your leadership attention aligns with what truly matters. This tool helps you spot where loyalty has turned into inertia, where opportunity is being neglected, and where your time could create the highest return.

Use this map quarterly or before major transitions. Review it when you feel stretched thin or disconnected. Each time, ask two questions: Does this map reflect my strategy? Does it reflect my values?

How to Apply

- **List your top twenty relationships:** those who consume most of your time and those most critical to your company's future.
- **Map each one on the grid:** Strategic Value (low to high) versus Energy Investment (low to high).
- **Check balance across arenas:** Bosses, Team, Collaborators, Community, Customers, and You. Are any neglected?
- **Spot misalignments:** Who gets too much time versus who deserves more?
- **Commit to six actions:** three to reengage or elevate, and three to reset, delegate, or let go.

Prioritization is never perfect—it's a moving target. Even with a clear map, emotions, habits, and shifting circumstances will test your discipline. The real work isn't drawing boxes, but putting the insight into action. As you begin to clarify where your energy truly belongs, you'll also begin to notice what gets in the way. And that's where we turn next: the common obstacles that quietly pull leaders off course.

COMMON OBSTACLES AND HOW TO AVOID THEM

Even with the best intentions, prioritization gets messy. The calendar fills, the inbox overflows, and slowly your time begins to take a life of its own. Most CEOs don't lose focus because they lack discipline—they lose it because the noise feels urgent and the important often feels optional.

Here are a few traps to watch for:

- **The Guilt Trap:** You keep meeting with people out of loyalty, not logic. They helped you once, and you feel you owe them. But loyalty doesn't mean unlimited access. The longer you operate from guilt, the more you rob your future to pay for your past.
- **The Familiarity Bias:** You default to relationships that feel easy or affirming. It's natural—you get quick energy from those conversations. But the relationships that grow the business are often the ones that stretch you. Comfort can quietly become complacency.
- **The "One More Thing" Syndrome:** You tell yourself you'll focus on priorities once this quarter ends, once the new hire starts, once the deal closes. But prioritization is not something you do later, it's how you get through now.
- **The All-Access Habit:** You make yourself too available. Everyone gets time, which means no one gets your best time. Accessibility isn't the same as impact.

Prioritization gives shape to your leadership. It focuses your time, sharpens your intent, and ensures your energy is spent where it truly matters. But once you've chosen where to invest, another challenge begins: staying objective about whether those investments are actually paying off. Over time, relationships evolve, strategies shift; the people and partnerships that mattered most a year ago may not hold the same weight tomorrow.

That's where the final discipline comes in: *evaluate.* In the next chapter, we'll explore how great CEOs build a system of reflection and review—so their relationships stay aligned with reality, not memory.

QUICK RELATIONSHIP AUDIT

Ask yourself:

- Do my calendar and my priorities tell the same story?
- Which relationships once mattered deeply but no longer align with our direction?
- Who are the people or partners I should be spending more time with—but haven't?
- Have I been avoiding certain relationships because they challenge or stretch me?
- Do my team, board, and clients understand what relationships I've chosen to prioritize—and why?

KEY TAKEAWAYS

- **Prioritization is the leadership discipline.** Prioritization is how you turn good intentions into focused impact.
- **Your time and attention are your most valuable forms of capital.** Invest them where they compound, not where they comfort.
- **High Payoff Activities reveal where your unique contribution truly moves the business forward.** Take account of your time and be honest about how your actions can have the biggest impact on the business.
- **Relationship Zones help you clarify where each connection belongs.** This tool shows you how much access and energy each relationship deserves.
- **The Relationship Prioritization Map transforms reflection into action.** This tool exposes the gap between where your time goes and where your strategy needs it to be.
- **The hardest part of prioritization isn't saying no to others.** The hardest part is saying no to the parts of yourself that crave being liked, needed, or involved.

Chapter 11

EVALUATE

The trip was supposed to be a celebration.

After years of expansion, the family business was thriving—new markets, new ventures, new legitimacy on the horizon. The CEO had flown to an exotic Caribbean island to meet with investors and longtime partners. There were cigars, champagne, and promises of even greater success ahead.

But as the toasts began, something didn't sit right. His most trusted partner—the one who'd been with the family since his father first built the company—was making commitments that carried more risk than sense. He spoke of outsized returns, expanded territories, and unseen control. The CEO listened, polite but quiet, his expression unreadable. He'd known this man his entire life. But tonight, he realized they no longer wanted the same thing.

That night, alone in his suite, he began taking stock. Of his older brother, still on the payroll, but now a drain, unreliable and reckless with the business they had built. Of his trusted advisor—loyal and sharp, but too cautious, too attached to the past. The company's strategy was evolving, and so were the people around him. Relationships that once fueled growth were now holding it back.

The next morning, the celebration continued as planned. The CEO carried on as if everything were the same, but inside, the decisions were already made. Some relationships would have to change. Others would have to end. The business was moving forward—and so would its alliances.

The CEO in that Caribbean hotel wasn't a modern executive. It was Michael Corleone—the head of the Corleone family in *The Godfather Part II*. In that moment, he was doing what every great leader eventually must: evaluating which relationships still serve the mission—and which ones belong to another era.

Michael's moment in Havana captures what every CEO eventually faces—the realization that relationships don't stay fixed, even when they were once foundational. Time, strategy, and circumstance change the equation. What worked before can become a liability if you don't stop to reassess it. That's what "Evaluate" is about—taking deliberate inventory of your most important relationships, understanding how they've evolved, and having the courage to adjust before misalignment becomes a problem.

WHY *EVALUATING* MATTERS

Every relationship changes over time—some evolve, others erode. Strategies shift, markets move, people change roles, and priorities realign. The leader who fails to recognize these shifts risks steering the company with yesterday's map. *Evaluate* is the discipline of noticing change before it becomes a crisis. It's about understanding that no relationship—no matter how loyal, historic, or successful—stays static. As the landscape of your business moves, your relationships must move with it.

In relational leadership, *Evaluate* means taking deliberate time to reflect and refine. It's not about suspicion or cynicism; it's about curiosity and awareness. Just as you review financial performance or operational metrics, you should regularly review the state of your key relationships. What has changed for them? What has changed for you?

A client's priorities may shift after an acquisition. A trusted advisor might lose influence inside their organization. A board member's risk tolerance might harden with market volatility. If you're not paying attention, you'll act as if nothing has changed—until the relationship stops working.

Evaluation is how you stay aligned with reality. It forces you to look outward—to the market, to your stakeholders, to the broader forces shaping your environment—and inward, to your own evolving goals. Evaluation needs to become a continuous mindset. The best CEOs don't just react to drift—they anticipate it. They build systems, rhythms, and networks that keep them informed about subtle shifts before they show up as surprises.

Recognizing that relationships evolve is only the first step. The real challenge is building a rhythm for how you evaluate them—what to look for, how often to check in, and how to translate what you find into action. The following tools will help you do that: practical ways to notice shifts, assess fit, and keep your most important relationships aligned with where you—and your business—are headed.

HOW TO PRACTICE IT: TOOLS AND TACTICS

Over the years—through my own leadership journey and working with other CEOs—I've learned that relationships are dynamic. They need to be evaluated with the same rigor you apply to reviewing your company's financials and key performance indicators (KPIs). There's no single formula for how to do it right, but there is a discipline to doing it consistently. These tools are simply the ones that have helped me stay proactive, honest, and balanced in my own evaluation rhythm. Use them as a framework, then adapt them to fit your world.

The Three Tools:

- **The Relationship Pulse:** A quick, regular rhythm for checking the "vital signs" of your key relationships. Build it into your normal operating cadence—executive meetings, board sessions, client check-ins—to see who has influence, who's fading, and how those shifts affect your goals.

- **Managing the Shift:** A deeper strategic review. Step back to see how your network is changing, where new risks or opportunities are emerging, and which relationships may need to be redefined or rebalanced.
- **Future Fit:** A forward-looking discipline. Anticipate which relationships will change next—retirements, acquisitions, leadership transitions, new players entering your orbit—so you can prepare now instead of reacting later.

Each of these tools helps you look at relationships through time: the present, the past, and the future. Together, they keep your relational leadership strategy as current as your business strategy. Let's review the first tool in this tool kit, the Relationship Pulse.

THE RELATIONSHIP PULSE

One of the habits I've seen in great leaders—and worked to build myself—is developing a rhythm for noticing what's changing in the relationships that matter most. It starts with curiosity and a commitment to continuously ask questions. This awareness needs to be built into your normal cadence in your key meetings.

If you go back to one of the tools we introduced in Chapter 2, The Team, we outlined how your weekly Priorities Meeting should be run. Part of the weekly agenda includes getting customer and employee data. Your team should be feeding you information, and over time you should be getting information about some of your key relationships. But, the awareness and questions should be part of almost all of your meetings and across all key relationships. You can't assume that all is good and will always be good.

The Relationship Pulse is about staying tuned in to what's happening right now. Who's engaged? Who's drifting? Who suddenly has influence they didn't have before? When you make this kind of awareness a routine part of how you run your meetings, manage your calendar, and talk to your team, you spot movement before it turns into a surprise.

The pulse doesn't require you to have yet another meeting. It's a habit you weave into the ones you already have.

Over time, this rhythm builds intuition. It's how CEOs stay ahead of the game and make better decisions about where to focus.

How to Apply

- Add a five-minute Relationship Pulse slot to your weekly executive meeting agenda.
- During one-on-ones, ask your direct reports who they've been hearing from—and who's gone quiet.
- When prepping for important meetings with an important relationship, take a moment to discuss tone and energy, not just numbers.
- Encourage your team to flag changes in the relationship landscape—shifts in sentiment, influence, or enthusiasm.

Checking the pulse helps you sense movement early. Once you see a shift, awareness alone isn't enough—you have to decide what to do about it. That's where the next tool comes in: managing the shift.

MANAGING THE SHIFT

When I look back at the early days of launching Apollo Bank, I had a lot going for me—experience as a leader and entrepreneur, great relationships with potential clients and investors, and a sound strategy. What I didn't have was firsthand experience running a bank.

That's where Richard Dailey came in.

Richard looked like he'd been born to run a bank. Decades older than me, calm under pressure, and credible in every room, he had already built one successful bank in the same market. He'd spent his career at Wells Fargo and had the polish that comes from working across Europe and Latin America. When we met, it wasn't through a long courtship. We barely knew each other. But from the start, we both sensed we could build something important together.

In those early days, Richard was my translator. He helped me navigate a regulated industry where words, timing, and tone mattered as much as capital. He wasn't just a mentor—he lent me his credibility. When I walked into meetings with regulators and investors, the fact that Richard was beside me spoke louder than any business plan ever could.

We built Apollo Bank side by side. And then, over time, the relationship began to shift—naturally, and without friction. As the company grew, I was taking on more responsibility as CEO and chairman. Richard, who could have held tight to his original role, showed remarkable grace. He transitioned from co-founder to president, then eventually from president to a board member.

Each change was smooth—no power struggles, no awkward conversations. Why? Because we were intentional. We checked in not just about the business, but about the relationship itself. We made room for evolution.

That experience taught me something I've seen play out again and again with other CEOs: Longevity doesn't mean sameness. The best professional relationships—especially between founders, executives, and early partners—move through seasons. The healthiest ones evolve before they break.

Richard and I stayed aligned because we talked openly about change. We didn't wait for tension or resentment to force a conversation. Even now, years later, he remains a sounding board and friend. He shows up when it matters, offers perspective when I ask, and respects the space when I don't. That kind of relationship is rare—and it's built on trust strong enough to survive transition.

Every CEO will face this moment. Someone who helped you get started won't always be the person who helps you scale. The question is: Can the relationship evolve? If not, can it still have value in a different role?

Most CEOs underestimate how quietly relationships can drift out of alignment. It doesn't happen with a blowup or betrayal. It happens with small changes—new titles, new pressures, new ambitions—that slowly change what people need from one another.

These shifts happen across all the relationship arenas. I'm sure you've had a key contact at one of the companies you interact with get demoted and now you have to work with someone new; or you have to work with someone who replaced someone you considered more than a collaborator or vendor, but a friend. The best leaders make these conversations a normal part of doing business. They don't wait until there's friction. They say, "We've grown, and so has the business. Let's talk about how we keep this relationship strong through the next stage." That tone—respectful, proactive, and open—keeps relationships from hardening into resentment or fading into irrelevance.

There's another truth most CEOs eventually learn: Not every relationship ends on equal footing. Some people can't—or won't—adapt to the next version of your company. That doesn't mean you were wrong to work with them; it just means the season has changed. The challenge is to lead those transitions without drama or bitterness. It's one of the hardest parts of leadership, but it's also one of the most defining.

Managing the shift comes down to stewardship. It's protecting what works, repurposing what can still add value, and letting go of what no longer fits. The relationships that endure are the ones flexible enough to evolve as you do.

HOW TO APPLY

- **Build check-ins into your routine.** Shifts rarely announce themselves. Use your one-on-ones, board updates, and key client meetings to check the temperature of relationships. Ask: *What's changed? What's next? What do they need from me now that's different from before?*
- **Name the change.** When you sense the dynamic evolving, bring it

up directly—without blame or emotion. Say something like, "We've both grown since we started working together. Let's talk about how this relationship needs to evolve." Naming the shift normalizes it.

- **Revisit roles and boundaries.** Growth often means redefining who does what. Don't wait until overlap or confusion sets in. Clarify where you still add value—and where others can take the lead.
- **Keep the dignity of the past intact.** When a relationship needs to change form—especially one that helped you get started—honor its history. Gratitude softens transition. People remember how you treat them when the season changes.
- **Use a simple framework: Reinforce, reset, or release.** Decide if the relationship should be reinforced (deepen trust), reset (redefine terms), or released (step back respectfully). The goal isn't to protect every bond—it's to preserve alignment.

Managing the shift is leadership in motion. It's how you stay aligned with strategy while staying loyal to your values. If managing the shift is about staying attuned to what's changing now, *future fit* is about anticipating what's coming next. The best CEOs don't just react to relational changes—they see them forming on the horizon. They know which leaders are nearing retirement, which clients are grooming successors, which partners are quietly building new ambitions. They prepare for these evolutions early, while trust and communication are still strong.

FUTURE FIT

When Wim Wenders set out to make *Paris, Texas* in the early 1980s, he wasn't just chasing a story—he was betting on a web of relationships he'd been quietly building for years.

By then, Wenders was already one of Europe's most admired filmmakers, known for *The American Friend* and *Wings of Desire*. But he longed to capture the emotional geography of America—the vast landscapes, the loneliness, the search for connection. Though European by birth, Wenders had been embraced by a new generation of American film students. At UCLA he'd lectured, screened films, and mentored young directors. He kept in touch with several of them, knowing that when the time came to shoot in the US, these relationships would be his first bridge.

When *Paris, Texas* finally got its green light, Wenders immediately drew on those connections. He hired a handful of UCLA students to scout locations across Arizona and Texas. They returned with photos, local contacts, and notes that would shape the film's dusty, sun-baked realism. Wenders hadn't hired them because of pedigree, but because he trusted their passion and perspective.

He took the same relational approach to the film's creative core. The initial script came from playwright Sam Shepard, whose gift for spare dialogue and rural poetry was a perfect match for Wenders's vision. But Wenders knew Shepard's calendar was packed with theater projects, and he quietly prepared for that eventuality. When Shepard had to leave mid-production, Wenders already had a plan—and a person. He brought in L.M. Kit Carson to finish the script, a collaborator he'd built trust with long before the need arose. The handoff was smooth, the story deepened, and the production kept moving.

Music, too, demanded adaptability. Wenders had cultivated a friendship with Bob Dylan, and the two had discussed Dylan scoring the film. But as production tightened and Dylan's schedule (and fee) became prohibitive, Wenders pivoted again. He reached out to Ry Cooder, whose slide-guitar work infused the film with a haunting intimacy that became its emotional heartbeat. That collaboration sparked a creative partnership that would later lead to *Buena Vista Social Club*, earning both men global acclaim.

When *Paris, Texas* premiered at Cannes in 1984, it won the Palme d'Or (widely considered the highest artistic honor for a film) and stunned audiences. Yet beneath the accolades was a lesson in foresight. Wenders hadn't just assembled talent; he'd built a network of adaptable relationships that allowed the film to weather every shift—creative, logistical, and financial.

He didn't wait for things to fall apart to find new partners. He anticipated the pivots. He forecasted his future fit.

For CEOs, that's the essence of relational strategy. Markets change, priorities evolve, and people move on. The leaders who thrive are the ones who build a pipeline of future relationships of individuals who can step up before they're needed, not after the storm hits.

Wenders knew that challenges and unforeseen problems were always right around the corner. Every contingency, every collaborator, every creative pivot was supported by relationships he'd nurtured long before he needed them. That's what makes "future fit" such a powerful discipline for leaders. You don't need to predict the future; you just need to stay connected to the people who can help you adapt when it arrives. Below are some of the ways I have found to best keep that practice alive in your own leadership—to help you anticipate shifts, build your bench, and prepare your relationships for the next chapter before the moment demands it.

How to Apply

- **Name the likely pivots.** Identify the three to five areas where your strategy could realistically shift this year—new regulations, key client transitions, leadership succession, or capital raises. For each, name one future ally to start cultivating now: the deputy GC at your regulator, the heir apparent at a major client, or the next-generation leader at a partner firm.
- **Build your bench.** For every mission-critical relationship, identify (and meet) a "second." Don't wait for turnover or crisis to start grooming relational successors.
- **Create a low-friction first touch.** Don't wait for a need or emergency to connect. Invite a prospective collaborator to a small roundtable, ask for feedback on a memo, or cohost a short event. Keep the interaction light but genuine—build the relationship before you need it.
- **Track inflection points.** During quarterly reviews, scan for upcoming retirements, leadership changes, mergers, or political

shifts. Wherever a seat might soon change, start building trust with the likely successor.

- **Invest in adjacent creators.** Like Wenders with Ry Cooder, cultivate people whose craft complements yours and could become central in a future chapter—perhaps a data partner who could power your next product, or a community leader who could anchor a new market.

Even with the best intentions, forecasting relationships isn't easy. The future rarely unfolds on schedule, and even your best instincts will sometimes miss the mark. What matters most is staying alert to the warning signs—the small gaps between what you expected and what's actually happening. Before we close this chapter, let's look at a few common obstacles that trip up even the most disciplined leaders, and how to avoid them.

COMMON OBSTACLES AND HOW TO AVOID THEM

No leader gets this perfectly right. Relationships evolve faster than calendars or dashboards can track. The goal isn't perfection, but awareness. What separates the best CEOs is their ability to notice the drift early and correct course before trust or timing is lost.

- **Waiting too long to reassess.** Most CEOs know a relationship needs to change long before they act on it. But loyalty, optimism, or simple busyness delay the decision. By the time you act, the damage is done—trust has eroded or opportunities have passed.
- **Ignoring the secondary network.** A relationship can shift even if the primary person hasn't. Maybe your contact retires, gets promoted, or loses influence—and you fail to build ties with their successors or deputies.
- **Overreacting to change.** Sometimes leaders swing too far the other way—overhauling relationships at the first sign of tension. Not every shift is a fracture. Some just need clarity or a reset.

- **Failing to communicate the shift.** You may evolve a relationship quietly in your head, but if you don't tell the other person, they'll feel blindsided or devalued. Silence breeds resentment.

If you've worked through each part of CARPE, you've already begun the real work of relational leadership. **You've learned to** *Connect* **with intention,** *Align* **around shared purpose,** *Respond* **with deliberate action,** *Prioritize* **where your time and presence matter most,** and *Evaluate* **as things inevitably change.** Together, these practices form more than a framework—they create a rhythm. The best leaders don't move through relationships in a straight line. They circle through them—checking in, adjusting, refining, and reconnecting again.

Because in the end, it always comes back to relationships. They are the work, the legacy, and the story worth telling.

QUICK RELATIONSHIP AUDIT

Ask yourself:

- Which of my key relationships have changed the most in the last year—and have I adjusted to those shifts?
- Who has quietly gained or lost influence in my world without me noticing?
- Where am I still operating on old assumptions about loyalty, access, or alignment?
- Which relationships need a pulse check, and which need a reset?
- What future transitions—retirements, successions, leadership shifts—should I be preparing for now?
- Who deserves a simple, genuine conversation to realign expectations or express appreciation?

KEY TAKEAWAYS

- **Relationships evolve.** The circumstances, goals, and people that once fit perfectly may not fit the same way tomorrow.
- **Evaluation is proactive, not reactive.** Don't wait for a problem to recognize change; build regular review into your leadership rhythm.
- **The best leaders recalibrate with clarity and grace.** When a relationship needs to shift, communicate it clearly and respectfully.
- **Forecasting is part of leadership.** Cultivate the relationships you'll need next year, not just the ones serving you now.
- **CARPE is a cycle, not a checklist.** Connecting, Aligning, Responding, Prioritizing, and Evaluating form a continuous loop. When you evaluate well, you set the stage to reconnect—stronger and smarter than before.

CONCLUSION

When I started writing this book, I thought it would be about strategy. But what emerged was something far more personal—and far more powerful.

Because in the end, leadership isn't about being the smartest or the most visionary or even the hardest working. It's about being the most connected. Not in a superficial way. Not in a "who you know" kind of way. But in a deep, intentional, resilient way.

It's all about relationships.

If you're a CEO, a founder, or a leader of any kind, you're not just managing an organization. You're managing a network of people who trust you, follow you, challenge you, support you, and rely on you.

Your results come from your relationships. Period.

That's why this work matters so much.

Part I of this book laid out the six essential relationships every CEO must master:

- **The Bosses:** How to identify who is really "above you" and how to manage up, earn trust, and avoid being blindsided.

- **The Team:** How to build, align, and lead the people who drive execution.
- **The Collaborators:** How to work with key allies who don't sit inside your org chart but might have a bigger impact than those who do.
- **The Community:** How to lead publicly—through media, government, and institutions.
- **The Customer:** How to listen deeply, deliver consistently, and respond with purpose.
- **Yourself:** How to manage your time, energy, and mindset to lead effectively.

These are not categories. They're people—each with their own hopes, pressures, and influence on your mission. They are the ecosystem of your leadership.

Part II introduced the CARPE framework, a simple but powerful system to help you lead those relationships with clarity, consistency, and care:

- **Connect:** Find ways to build real trust.
- **Align:** Uncover shared goals and incentives.
- **Respond:** Act with presence and purpose.
- **Prioritize:** Focus on the few that matter most.
- **Evaluate:** Revisit, reassess, and adapt.

These five disciplines work like muscles. The more you use them, the stronger your relationships—and your leadership—become.

I've learned after decades of leading, coaching, and building that none of this is static. Relationships breathe. They shift. They evolve. Some will fade. Others will deepen. The work is not to hold them all tightly, but to stay awake—to stay present enough to see when a connection needs to be renewed, when alignment needs to be rebuilt, and when it's time to let something go with grace.

If there's one action I want you to take after finishing this book, it's this: *Choose one key relationship right now.* A relationship that truly matters to your success—or your peace of mind. Maybe it's a board member you've grown distant from. A client you've taken for granted. A direct report who's waiting for more of you. Or maybe it's the relationship with yourself that's been put last for too long.

Start there.

Use CARPE.

Connect intentionally. Align clearly. Respond deliberately. Prioritize honestly. Evaluate often.

You don't have to do it all at once. Just start—today—with one conversation that matters.

Because when you do, something powerful happens: Clarity returns. Energy follows. Trust builds. And that single act of attention begins to ripple outward—through your company, your community, your life.

Leadership isn't a solo performance. It's a symphony of relationships, tuned over time through empathy, courage, and consistency. And when you get it right, it's beautiful.

So yes, *seize the day*—but more importantly, *seize the relationship.*

If this book has sparked ideas, reflections, or even challenges you're working through, I'd love to hear from you. Visit www.arriolaco.com or send me a note on LinkedIn, linkedin.com/in/eddy-arriola-9ba0255/. Tell me what you're building, what you're learning, and how you're using these tools.

We grow through each other. We lead through each other. And we find meaning—always—in relationships.

Because at the end of the day, and at the end of every great story—*it's all about relationships.*

ACKNOWLEDGMENTS

Writing a book is harder than I ever imagined—and far more rewarding than I ever expected.

But why write a book in the first place?

When I first got my driver's license, the first place I drove wasn't to a friend's house, a party, or a football game—it was straight to the corner of Aragon and Salzedo in Coral Gables, to the original location of the local independent bookstore Books & Books. I love books. I believe books are sacred. I wanted to give something back to the world of readers, writers, and booksellers. Thank you to the world of books for all the joy you have brought into my life.

It's all about relationships, right?

Well, I'd like to acknowledge some important relationships in my life.

My book journey begins with my mom—thank you for passing along your love of reading and for holding all those books I've kept stored at your house for so many years. You've been a lifetime of support and love.

My fascination with the machine of business and the example of leadership is attributable to my dad. Thank you for showing me the impact a CEO can have on people and the community. I love you.

To my wonderful siblings, who were my first teammates and constant collaborators: Ricky–thank you for your inspiration and for pushing me to be better every day. Danny—many of the ideas in this book are ones we've discussed, debated, and put into practice over decades; thank you. Franky—thank you for your thoughts and experiences around writing and creativity, and for all the book and movie recommendations. Luly—thank you for encouraging me to lead by example. Our relationships are the roots of everything that has grown since we were kids.

I am deeply indebted to the many friends who have shaped my life—especially two people without whose encouragement and support I never would have finished this book: Matt Adler, who knew how important this project was to me, and Matt Kuttler, who has been my coach and sounding board for so many years (the Jim Harbaugh story is for you).

To my YPO Forums—the old, the new, and my banking forum—thank you: Henry Nahmad, Wicho Hernandez, Joe Rubinzstain, Matt Greer, Don Schenker, and Manny Balani; Pablo Montesano, Walter Gonzalez, Ryan Moul, Ed Boucas, and Diego Ojeda; Pat Ryan, Austin Buerge, Matt Michaelis, Jim Walker, and AJ Antongiovanni. And to the entire YPO and EO communities that have been foundational in my business and personal development.

To the teams and relationships built over the years at Avanti, Inktel, Apollo Bank, Seacoast Bank, the Inter-American Foundation, and the Federal Home Loan Bank of Atlanta. To my classmates and teachers at Christopher Columbus High School, Boston College, and HBS OPM 35.

To two incredible individuals who started out as my teachers and became lifelong friends—John Lynskey and Deepak Malhotra. You are both celebrated authors in your own right. John, thank you for your frequent check-ins. Deepak, your encouragement and example led me to put pen to paper—and keep my butt in the seat.

To so many other friends I can't thank enough—or risk forgetting to mention: David Isenberg, Lowell Harrison, Dr. Carter Burrus,

Tadd Schwartz, Chuck Shaffer, Curt Miner, Gil Bonwitt, Nick Molina, Carlos Herrera, Jonathan Liguori, Carlos Modia, Richard Dailey, Tania Dominguez, Robby Elias, Paloma Adams-Allen, Bob Kaplan, Sara Aviel, Michael Tobin, Jim Lowry, Bill Heffernan, Mary Albanese, Miguel Rishmague, Leslie Rozencwaig, Jeff Levine, Adrienne Arsht, Brother Kevin Handibode, David McCombie, Dr. Aldrich Chan, Pablo Gonzalez, Juan Carlos Iturregui, Kelly Ryan, Lou Viada, Jason Manganaro, and Kevin Durkin. Thank you to the Lane Family (which includes the Smiths, Messinas, and Kleins).

To the guys who aren't blood-related but I consider brothers: Jason Schlenker, Luis Gonzalez, and Ben Teasdale.

To the CEOs I've coached, worked alongside, and learned from—you are the reason this book exists. Your challenges, breakthroughs, and raw honesty gave me the insight and inspiration to write this. Thank you for trusting me.

Thanks to everyone on the Scribe team for supporting this project, reading early drafts, and keeping me focused when I tried to overcomplicate things. Special thanks to Rikki Jump and her great follow-up; Katie Lathrop, the ever-patient publishing manager; Aleks Mendel for coaching me in those early days; Kathleen McIntosh for getting this book back on track; and Anna Dorfman, for her amazing cover design. And of course, the man behind the curtain, Mark Chait.

A special thanks to my children, Ben and Grace. Not only are you amazing humans and the best kids a parent could ever dream of, but you are wise and insightful. Ben—thank you for being my early reader and for your many editing suggestions. Grace—thank you for your marketing insight and perspective.

To my wife, Katie—for your love, patience, wisdom, and unwavering belief in this work. You've lived the truth of this book with me every day.

And finally, to you—the reader: I hope this book helps you show up in your leadership with more clarity, more humility, and more strength.

ABOUT THE AUTHOR

EDDY ARRIOLA is a seasoned entrepreneur, CEO, board member, and advisor to CEOs, known for building successful companies and guiding leaders through moments of growth, transition, and transformation. He is the founder and former chairman and CEO of Apollo Bank, which launched during the great financial crisis and grew into one of the most respected banks in the Southeast, ultimately completing a successful exit to a publicly traded company. Under his leadership, Apollo Bank earned national recognition for innovation, corporate culture, and service to the community.

In addition to founding multiple companies and advising high-growth startups, Eddy has served on the boards of private and public companies across sectors—from fintech and healthcare to banking and real estate. His experience includes board service with gMed (acquired by Modernizing Medicine), TotalBank (acquired by Banco Popular de España), and two SEC-registered institutions: Seacoast Bank (NASDAQ: SBCF), the Federal Home Loan Bank of Atlanta, Linkvest, and Plug&Lend. He also served two terms on the board of the Federal Reserve Bank of Atlanta (Miami Branch) and was appointed by President Barack Obama—confirmed by the US

Senate—as chairman of the Inter-American Foundation, a position he continued to hold under the Trump and Biden administrations.

Eddy is a nationally recognized speaker, author, a longtime member of YPO and EO, and a trusted advisor to private equity firms and executive teams. His leadership reflects a lifelong commitment to learning, integrity, and helping others grow.

Today, he is an active advisor to companies and CEOs who want to become better leaders, scale their businesses, and lead with greater clarity and confidence. Through his firm, Arriola & Co., he advises CEOs and executive teams on leadership, strategy, and culture. He also serves as a trusted coach, helping leaders navigate complex decisions and high-stakes relationships.

He was born and raised in Miami, Florida, and is a graduate of Boston College and Christopher Columbus High School.

This is his first book.